DEBUNKED

CASEY LYTLE

Publisher Mike Sanders
Art Director and Designer William Thomas
Senior Editor Alexandra Andrzejewski
Editor Christopher Stolle
Proofreaders Bill Bowers & Polly Zetterberg
Indexer Celia McCoy

First American Edition, 2022
Published in the United States by DK Publishing
6081 E. 82nd St., Suite 400, Indianapolis, IN 46250

22 23 24 25 26 10 9 8 7 6 5 4 3 2 1
001-332273-SEP2022

Published in the United States
by Dorling Kindersley Limited.

Library of Congress Catalog Number: 2022934275
ISBN: 978-0-7440-6273-1

Printed and bound in United States of America

For the curious
www.dk.com

CONTENTS

Introduction 7

1 The Spectrum of Conspiracy Theories & the Project Management Approach 11

2 The Psychology of Conspiracy 17

3 Chemtrails 37

4 The Kennedy Assassination 45

5 The Moon Landing Hoax 59

6 Area 51 & Extraterrestrial UFOs 69

7 September 11, 2001 83

8 Mass Shootings, False Flags & the Truthers 101

9 QAnon & the 2020 Presidential Election 115

10 COVID-19 & the COVID Vaccines 131

11 The Deep State & Secretly Murdered Celebrities 153

12 Pop Culture Conspiracy Theories 185

Index 199

INTRODUCTION

CONSPIRACY THEORIES: WHY DO THEY FASCINATE US?

Why write a book about conspiracy theories? Because they've become so influential and spread to sometimes irrational extremes. Is there a way to separate the possible from the impossible? Yes. This book does that.

Conspiracy theories have been around forever. They flourish every time there's a national or cultural crisis, especially in times and places where people are suspicious of their own governments. As I'll discuss in the Chapter 1, these beliefs are fueled when real secret operations that have been carried out are revealed to the public despite efforts made to keep them secret.

Historically, conspiracy theorists were mostly small and isolated groups. Think of the Lone Gunmen as represented on the 1990s TV show *The X Files* and their own brief spin-off show. In the last couple decades, the internet has brought these conspiracy groups together and given them a much larger platform. The larger the platform, the more a belief can spread. Now there are conspiracy theories surrounding almost every major national or global event.

Conspiracy theories started to explode in the 1970s because of two real-world events: the Kennedy assassination and Watergate. Both cases resulted in many documents becoming declassified and many previously secret operations becoming public knowledge. As you can imagine, real cover-ups will open the door for beliefs in other secret operations that haven't yet become public knowledge. Does that mean every conspiracy theory is valid? Not at all. So how can you be an intelligent consumer of "alternative" theories? I hope to give you a hand there.

When I first began teaching a general psychology course, a frequent question I'd get from students was: "What causes people to believe in conspiracy theories and why do some people get so aggressive in defending their beliefs?" The interest and excitement in the class over these questions eventually led to "Psychology of Conspiracy Beliefs" becoming its own section in my psychology and sociology classes. This led to a second common question: "How can I cut through the bull and figure out which conspiracies could be true and which ones are completely ridiculous?" This question led to the format you'll find in this book: putting conspiracy theories on a spectrum from possible to impossible and using a project management approach to decide where on the spectrum they'd land.

What do I mean by "project management"? I mean considering the conspiracy from a practical standpoint and thinking about what it would take, step-by-step, to carry it out. How many people would be needed? What records would have to be fabricated? How many people would it take to infiltrate and fake those records? And, most importantly, what's the goal of the conspiracy and is the suggested conspiracy the best way you could think of to achieve the goal and expect success? Are there much easier ways to carry out the same goal that would involve fewer people and have a better chance of success? These are the questions conspiracy theorists avoid thinking about and these are the questions I'd ask the class as we brought up the conspiracy theories you'll find in these pages.

I've selected several popular and controversial conspiracy theories and dedicated a chapter to each one. In each chapter, we'll start with the official description of the event and then describe the conspiracy theories surrounding it. Then we'll take a practical approach to what might be required to carry out such a conspiracy and consider what the assumed goal of the conspiracy is.

If there's a wide spectrum of conspiracies (such as around the 9/11 attacks), I'll place them on the spectrum from possible to impossible and describe why they'd be at those points on the spectrum. (Did the Twin Towers really look like a controlled demolition? Would jet fuel have to melt steel for the towers to collapse? What would it take in hours and people to secretly plant enough explosives to bring the buildings down without being discovered and without being set off by the impact or fires from the planes?) I'll then include some of the alternative ways the goals could have been achieved in a more practical way that had a greater chance to succeed.

If your interest in conspiracy theories is the psychology behind why people believe them and cling to them so powerfully, I'll hit that right away in the chapters 1 and 2, where I lay out the project management approach we'll take in the book and the psychological foundations that make conspiracies so appealing as well as some of the real events that were initially covered up, suspected and speculated by conspiracy theorists, and later discovered to be true. After that, we'll dedicate each chapter to a breakdown of a specific event and the conspiracies around it.

By the end of *Debunked*, you'll be a more rational consumer of information and have a greater understanding of those who are drawn to these extreme conspiracy theories.

With that, let's buckle up and go for a ride!

CHAPTER 1

THE SPECTRUM OF CONSPIRACY THEORIES & THE PROJECT MANAGEMENT APPROACH

The Spectrum

When I put conspiracy theories on a spectrum from likely to unlikely or possible to impossible, the most frequent question I get from students is: "Are there any easy indicators of where a conspiracy falls on that spectrum?" The answers are "Yes" and "Sometimes."

As we'll see in later chapters, many conspiracies will start with a rational base and then be very subtle in sneaking irrational or impossible support into the argument. Part of what fuels this is the same cognition that allows us to use the suspension of disbelief to enjoy movies and books that sometimes violate the real world. On a rational level, we know the hero can't fall 10 floors from a building and simply roll around in pain for a moment and then 5 minutes later they're unhurt and active. But we set this aside so we can continue to enjoy the movie. The effect of movies and TV and their use of suspension of disbelief will play a large role when we talk about the 9/11 conspiracies, which rely heavily on our belief in fictionalized disasters (such as building collapses) we see in movies.

Other conspiracies will start with a claim that's false and use it as the foundation for the rest of the conspiracy. This is a logical fallacy known as the "false premise fallacy." It's unfortunately very common and very effective. For example, we could claim it's impossible for humans to travel to the moon because radiation would kill them; therefore, the moon landing had to be fake. The premise that radiation would kill travelers to the moon is false and thus can't invalidate the moon landing.

Frequently, a student will come up to me after class or come by my office and want to talk about a specific conspiracy we talked about in class they felt I didn't fully understand or grasp. One of these categories of conspiracy theories that will always cause an internal eye roll the moment I hear it: anything involving crisis actors. Rule of thumb: If a conspiracy involves crisis actors, it's most likely on the impossible side of the spectrum.

Why? Think about what it would involve. The Sandy Hook shooting is frequently seen by conspiracy theorists as an example of crisis actors being used to portray victims, survivors, or the family and friends of the victims. That event was in 2012 and the victims' families are still being accused of being crisis actors. The entire premise of someone agreeing to be a crisis actor requires they'll play this part for the rest of their lives and the architects of the plan are confident not a single one of them will ever come clean and expose the truth.

That violates several of the key criteria we're going to set for an effective conspiracy: Maximize the chances of keeping it secret by involving as few people as possible.

The Project Management Approach

When thinking about the validity of a conspiracy, think of yourself as a member of a secret group that wants to carry out a secret plan without the public discovering it and with the greatest chance of success. This is what I mean when I say we take a project management approach to conspiracy theories. What would you have to do, step-by-step, to carry it out?

Here are some questions to think about when addressing a conspiracy:

- What's the motive for the conspiracy?
- What's the goal of the conspiracy?
- What's the easiest way to achieve the goal without being discovered?
- How many people would it take to carry it out (while maximizing the chances of avoiding leaks)?
- What materials would it take?
- How long would it take to put it together?
- Would public records need to be altered or created to back it up?

And ultimately, with whatever conspiracy you consider:

- Before carrying it out, would the conspiracy look like it had a high likelihood of success?
- Would there be an easier way to do it that would achieve the same goal with less effort and a better chance of success?

On the surface, it seems this kind of approach should make it difficult for anyone to believe in any of the more complex conspiracy theories (like secretly planting explosives throughout two skyscrapers to carry out a controlled demolition or staging a mass shooting with crisis actors), but this is where suspension of disbelief comes into play. Two of the most common ways people will ignore the problem of the details is to completely dismiss them with statements like "They have ways," "You don't know what they're capable of doing," or "That's what they want you to think."

What's the key similarity in all these? The omnipotent "they" who are conveniently capable of anything and possess technology that's being hidden from the general public. But for some reason, "they" can't manage to put together a plan that can't be exposed by a single YouTube video.

This dismissal of detail isn't unique to conspiracy theories. Propaganda has always used it in creating fear by establishing an enemy with little or no proof the person or group is a real threat. Few Americans sought verification during the Cold War or the Red Scare of the 1950s sought verification that most Soviet citizens were atheists or lived in impoverished conditions with the military roaming the streets to suppress them or that Soviet citizens hated everyone in prosperous countries and wanted them all dead. Propaganda encouraged most people to buy into the fear of the Soviet Union, and from there, we were willing to accept anything else that painted the threat as genuine. Conspiracy theories grow from a similar base: Once you're suspicious of the government or the superrich and believe they want to harm or control you, you're more likely to believe anything about them that would support that view.

And here we have our first big problem: Do you have a friend, relative, or loved one who holds some odd conspiracy theories and you're wondering how to get them to see the irrationality of it? It's very difficult. Our brains spend a lot of neural resources protecting our beliefs from outside influence, and the more emotionally important the beliefs are, the more energy your brain uses to protect them. If a conspiracy can be tied to any other perceived personal threat, it's then protected by the same mechanism that protects the perception of that threat. Not only that, but you might be perceived as part of the threat by trying to change the belief.

CHAPTER 2

THE PSYCHOLOGY OF CONSPIRACY

Before we hit the psychological factors that impact belief in conspiracy theories, let's look at the environmental influences. What do I mean by environmental influences? Verified, real-world events—of secret things going on that people are trying to cover up—that open the door to the belief. Anytime I dismiss the more outlandish conspiracy theories, believers of those theories will bring these up, as if by dismissing one theory, I'm dismissing them all.

Throughout later chapters, I'll bring up more realistic possibilities to some of the more outlandish conspiracy theories, but even then, it doesn't mean I believe or endorse any of them; I'm simply offering simpler alternatives to unrealistically complex conspiracies. So what are some real events that have occurred where people tried to keep them secret and made attempts to cover them up? That list could be its own book, but let's hit some highlights.

Watergate

It's one of the most famous political scandals and the reason the suffix *-gate* is attached to any scandal that gets media attention (such as Tom Brady's "deflate-gate" scandal surrounding underinflated footballs; Ariana Grande's "donut-gate" scandal after video surfaced of her licking unsold donuts at a shop; etc.).

On June 17, 1972, five men were arrested attempting to break into the Democratic National Committee (DNC) headquarters in the Watergate Office Building (hence the name Watergate to describe the scandal) in Washington, DC. To make a long story short, the burglars were later connected to officials of the Nixon administration and the Nixon re-election campaign committee. Evidence later confirmed President Nixon was aware of the attempt to collect information related to the upcoming presidential election—all of which led to House and Senate investigations and ultimately the resignation of President Nixon, who faced impeachment and likely removal from office by the Senate. Vice President Gerald Ford took office, and on September 8, 1974, he issued a full and unconditional pardon of Nixon, effectively immunizing him from prosecution for any part of the scandal.

Given our criteria for judging a conspiracy and cover-up, does Watergate fit the criteria as a good plan? Mostly yes.

The investigations ultimately led to 69 government officials being charged and 48 of them being convicted—most because of the attempts to cover up the Nixon administration's involvement in the burglary. Many fewer individuals were involved in planning and carrying out the burglary itself. In fact, it would've been a successful plan if not for one thing: failing to abort the second burglary attempt once they realized a guard found the tape placed on door latches of key entrances and offices to prevent them from locking.

The June 17th break-in wasn't the first attempt to get into the DNC headquarters. There was an earlier successful attempt on May 28th, during which listening devices were placed inside phones and pictures of key documents were taken. The second attempt was planned because some of the listening devices weren't working and some listening devices hadn't been placed on all the key phones. The first break-in was so successful in getting some pictures of documents, they felt it was worth a second attempt.

No one involved ever publicly stated the ultimate goal of the wiretapping and document collection. Were they looking for something specific or simply collecting information they could use against the Democratic Party? For our "What's the goal of the conspiracy?" criterion, we can only say data gathering. Does this plan meet that goal? Yes. Is the plan a good way to achieve the goal? It seems so.

The original group that brainstormed potential illegal activities to get information about the Democratic Party was G. Gordon Liddy, Jeb Magruder, Attorney General John Mitchell, and presidential counsel John Dean. Although details of the different suggested plans were never publicized, Mitchell shot down several plans as unrealistic, so they eventually simplified their plan to burglarize the DNC headquarters at the Watergate complex. This is very similar to what I do in class when we talk about conspiracy theories: We determine the goal of a conspiracy, then brainstorm different plans that are simpler and more realistic than the more complex and unrealistic conspiracy theories.

Did this plan—on paper anyway—look like it had a good chance of success? Yes. The first burglary went off without a hitch and wasn't discovered. The second one would've also been successful if not for a security guard noticing tape on the door latches, removing it, then later noticing the tape was there again. It was the replacing of the tape that was the key failure of the second burglary. Realistically, upon realizing the tape had been discovered and removed, the burglars should have aborted the second attempt. If they'd done this, no one would've been caught and this plan would never have been uncovered.

The second failure of the plan was one of overconfidence. They seemed to have no plan of what to do if the burglars were captured. Their attempts to cover it up were spontaneous and haphazard, with no indication there had been any advance plan of how to cover their tracks. One reason for this might have been their choice of hiring outsiders as four of the five burglars, therefore thinking if they were captured, there was nothing linking them back to any administration officials. But they didn't think this part all the way through because there was a money trail linking payments to the four burglars from administration officials.

Take a moment to think about another frequent claim of conspiracy theorists when it comes to the Deep State, a supposedly secret group of powerful global elite with nearly omnipotent ability to carry out and cover up conspiracies while at the same time being incapable of designing a plan that can't be easily discovered by someone sitting at their kitchen table watching YouTube videos.

If there truly is such a powerful Deep State, then yes, they could carry out incredible secret plans, but these plans would also be so well crafted, you'd never figure them out or even suspect them in the first place.

So do I personally believe secret things go on and are covered up? Yes. Do I think any of these can be easily deduced by conspiracy theorists looking at pictures or videos? No.

One of the frequent claims of conspiracy theorists is that the Deep State kills people who are loose ends, therefore reducing the chance someone will squeal. Do I think such a group would do this? Yes. Do I think it would be done the way many conspiracy theorists believe? Not at all.

We'll discuss that when we talk about the Kennedy assassination and the very public death of Lee Harvey Oswald, a killing that if it's part of a cover-up to keep him quiet makes absolutely no sense in the time, place, and manner in which it was carried out.

In the case of Watergate, wouldn't the conspirators have simply paid the burglars in cash, then arranged to have them knocked off after they were arrested so they wouldn't reveal anything? If these are the kinds of people who really want to cover their tracks, they'd absolutely make such plans.

Looking for Smart Conspiracies

Look at how many people believe Bill and Hillary Clinton are responsible for killing off political enemies to keep their records clean. If so, then why did Monica Lewinsky (caught in an affair with President Clinton) and Linda Tripp (who secretly recorded evidence of the misconduct) survive, considering how much damage they caused the Clintons? Given the political and social mood and biases of the time, it would've been easy to stage a murder–suicide and leave behind a note, supposedly from Lewinsky, about an age-gap, same-sex relationship gone bad and Tripp using Lewinsky's access to the president to create a smear campaign against Lewinsky and the president, leading Lewinsky in an act of depressive desperation and guilt to kill Tripp and herself. If the Clintons had such clandestine power to pull off the deaths of political enemies, wouldn't this one have been an easy choice?

When the United States was looking for justification to invade Iraq in 2003, President George W. Bush used the presence of weapons of mass destruction as a big selling point to get public and international support for the invasion. When initially no such weapons were found, it was a public humiliation for the president, including a very embarrassing moment when President Bush appeared to sarcastically look under a table for the weapons, belittling the sacrifices being made by servicepeople in harm's way. Again, if the government had the power to carry out almost any clandestine operation, it would've been remarkably simple to send in a very small special operations group ahead of the troops as Iraq fell to plant weapons for them to find, therefore avoiding the embarrassment.

Again, one of the ways conspiracy theorists ignore plot holes in the conspiracies is to throw the problems of logic, planning, and critical thinking into the magic buckets of "They have ways" and "You don't know what they're capable of." It's an erroneous way to backward-engineer a theory. They start with what they think happened, then create scenarios to support it without considering whether the scenarios make sense.

In this book, my goal is to get rid of components that don't make sense so we can have a better understanding of what's possible and what's not.

Watergate made sense. It was a plan that could have worked. It had only a few unforeseen flaws that blew it up. Obviously, it's in our category of "probable" because it really happened, but it's also in our category of plans that before being carried out would be seen as likely to succeed and initially didn't involve very many people. Most of the people involved were connected in some way with either the Nixon administration directly or the Republican Party in general; therefore, you could have confidence they'd keep it quiet. Again, it was the haphazard attempt at the cover-up after the arrests that resulted in more people getting involved, therefore more people who could potentially leak information. The most obvious and most damaging involvement was deputy FBI director William Mark Felt, who was revealed in 2005 to be the infamous informant "Deep Throat." He leaked information to *Washington Post* reporters Bob Woodward and Carl Bernstein, who exploded the case in the media, forcing political repercussions.

Project MK-Ultra

We follow with this story because the revelations from documents and recordings of Nixon and his associates during the Watergate investigations led CIA director Richard Helms to have most of the documents chronicling MK-Ultra destroyed. A filing error might be the only reason any documents survived.

MK-Ultra ran from 1953 to 1973 and is primarily known for experiments studying the effects of LSD on human subjects. It involved a wide range of experimentation, including not just LSD but also electroshock, sensory deprivation, and isolation as well as many other forms of torture. The purpose? To find methods of interrogation, manipulation, and mind control that would make it easy to get information out of people or control their behavior. Although many organizations and universities participated in these experiments, most didn't know they were being funded by the CIA and the military. When public institutions were used, the procedures were considered ethical for their time. The more unethical experiments were performed within the military, where information could be controlled and there was a greater chance of keeping the activities secret. The ultimate motivation was the suspicion that foreign enemies were using mind-control techniques. For example, was the Soviet Union using mind-control drugs and techniques to get people to defect and give up their secrets, and could US intelligence do the same?

Although there were rumors of the project for almost its entire duration, there was no solid evidence or media attention until 1974, when *The New York Times* began running articles voicing the conspiracy theories. Those reports led to official investigations by Congress, including the formation of the Church Committee led by Senator Frank Church and the Rockefeller Commission specifically investigating the CIA.

I mentioned earlier that most documents had been destroyed, but a "filing error" resulted in around 20,000 documents surviving because they'd been accidentally stored among financial records. In summer 1975, the commissions began releasing their findings, and in 1976, this led to President Ford issuing the first executive order limiting intelligence activities.

This is an important moment to hit another accusation that's often used to support unlikely conspiracy theories when reality and logic are getting in the way: the accusation that "Everyone is in on it" or the suspicion that almost all branches of government and the media are conspiring to keep something secret. In the case of MK-Ultra, it was the government itself that exposed the operation. If all government branches were in on it, the simple solution would've been to respond to the media attention with a simple denial, blowing off the accusations as "conspiracy theory paranoia." But they didn't. They investigated it, revealed it, and ultimately took action to prevent something similar from happening in the future.

Another rule of thumb is that the weaker a conspiracy theory and the more likely it is to be on our improbable or unlikely side of the spectrum, the more it's directly connected to how many different groups are suspected of being in on it. Too many hands in the pot (or cooks in the kitchen) violates one of our key criteria of a likely and successful conspiracy: limiting the number of people involved to reduce the chances the project will be revealed. For most of its run, the people behind Project MK-Ultra did a good job of keeping it secret because they were operating within structures (the military and the CIA) that already have an infrastructure in place to preserve the secrecy of information. Probably their greatest failure was in using outside resources (such as universities), which meant increasing the number of subjects who weren't under military or government control. Keep the experimentation limited to members of the military and the project might have been able to stay under the radar longer.

Supposedly, the project ended in 1973 and Executive Order 11905 of 1976 prevented it from resuming, but there are ongoing conspiracy theories that those measures were simply a way to silence the witnesses who had come forward and led the general public to believe the project was over. In fact, it was ongoing. I'm not saying this is true, but this would also fall under the umbrella of "probable and likely" because it would involve greater security around the operation and, learning from past mistakes, involve fewer people. It wouldn't surprise me at all if there was a breaking news story today about ongoing government experiments in mind control being exposed.

If you research Project MK-Ultra, you'll find a lot of other accusations as far as the people who took part, deaths resulting from the experiments, and even more heinous and unethical side projects associated with it. The reason I don't bring those up here is because those accusations came out after the public reveal of the project in the 1970s and you'll always find satellite theories popping up every time one theory is verified to be true. It's hard to absolutely prove many of these other accusations, but once you've set the stage to suspect the government (in this case, the military and the CIA), it makes it easier to convince people of other conspiracies, even when there's little or no evidence.

A side note to this: Another conspiracy in the 1970s is that the government stopped the experiments because they found LSD "opened" minds rather than making them vulnerable to brainwashing. It's no surprise this was pushed by the community of people who enjoyed the recreational use of psychedelics and wanted to see them as a counterculture drug or even as a weapon against government propaganda. Unfortunately, the truth is the exact opposite: LSD might be the best mind manipulation drug ever created, and even if it's not used today for experimentation, it might be currently used in interrogation. If I can guide and control your LSD experience, I can exert tremendous influence over what you think and do. LSD opens you to suggestion and any new information I give you during the experience will be perceived as a "revelation." That information will likely be encoded and consolidated into memory much more powerfully than a suggestion given to you without the influence of the drug.

How does MK-Ultra fit into our requirements for a good cover-up? It was carried out by agencies that already have good "information control" infrastructures in place and had a relatively isolated number of people who knew the true intentions of the program—and it was very well done. As noted earlier, it was a clerical error in filing the information that resulted in the program being revealed. If not for that simple error, it would've stayed secret to this day and be nothing more than an unproven conspiracy theory.

Operation Northwoods (1962)

In a nutshell, Operation Northwoods was a series of think tank proposals originating within the Department of

Defense and the Joint Chiefs of Staff. The goal was to stage terrorist attacks along the East Coast of the United States and blame them on Cuba as justification for the military invasion of Cuba to overthrow Fidel Castro. Some of the specific suggestions were attacks on Navy vessels and staged attacks on US facilities at Guantanamo Bay. Alternately, there were plans to covertly provoke Cuba into attacking US or allied interests, then using these attacks as the justification for open military action against the Cuban government.

There were many related proposals filed under different names: Operation Mongoose, Operation Bingo, Operation Dirty Trick, etc.—all of which shared the goal of finding a valid excuse to invade Cuba and remove Castro.

Why were none of these carried out? Because people along the chain of command seemed to have the same critical thinking and project management approach to secret operations that I'm using in this book. They realized carrying out such operations would involve too many people, creating too many opportunities for information to leak, and therefore the plans weren't viable. A Department of Defense report specifically noted that such operations should be limited to only the most highly trusted covert personnel.

If this was all so secret and was never acted upon, how did it become public knowledge? Simple answer: the investigations into who might have been involved in the assassination of President Kennedy. Given the tense relationship between the United States and Cuba, any documentation that could prove motive by Cuba would be part of that investigation and the Operation Northwoods documentation became part of that.

In November 1997, the John F. Kennedy Assassination Records Review Board released more than 1,500 pages of documents related to the assassination investigations and Operation Northwoods became public knowledge for the first time. In November 1998, more documents were released in a joint venture with CNN to coincide with a TV documentary they were producing on the Cold War. A more complete version of the Northwoods documents was released by the National Security Archive in April 2001.

Obviously, there are still conspiracies that float around this because it's unknown if the yet-unreleased documents related to the Kennedy investigations might reveal more. The planned release of more documents was delayed in 2018 by the Trump administration and again in 2021 by the Biden administration. The Biden administration claimed the delay was because of staffing issues surrounding the ongoing COVID pandemic, while the Trump administration delayed release for "national security concerns," which will obviously fuel conspiracy theorists asking: "What security concerns could still exist more than 50 years after the event?"

How well does Operation Northwoods fit into our requirements for a good cover-up? Very well. It originated within agencies that already have a secure infrastructure meant to prevent leaks of sensitive information, it involved a very small number of people (all of whom had high-level security clearances), and it would to this day still be unknown to the public if the records hadn't become part of the investigation into the Kennedy assassination. Like the others I've mentioned, it would still be an unproven conspiracy theory.

There have been many others, but these are a good sample of secret operations that unintentionally became public knowledge and helped spotlight that secret operations do occur and there are attempts to keep them secret; therefore, there must be others going on right now that we know nothing about. It's not hard to see how this opens the door for beliefs in conspiracy theories.

Let me give "honorable mention" to an event that's often brought up as a secret conspiracy but doesn't fit our criteria because at the time, there was no attempt to keep it secret: the Tuskegee Study (from 1932 to 1972), in which Black participants were intentionally given syphilis to study its progression and effects and weren't given medical treatment even after effective treatments were available. Not only was there no attempt to cover it up, but the people carrying out the "studies" also openly published their results several times without any attempt to keep it secret. The reason there was no outcry was because the media and the general public didn't care. If you want a stunning example of racism-based research and a deep-seated public attitude diminishing the value of a specific demographic, this is it. But for our purposes, it doesn't count as a conspiracy.

Cognitive & Psychological Influences

I've set the stage with some real-world events in which a small number of people attempted to carry out secret operations that were ultimately uncovered, reinforcing the idea that because secret things have been done in the past, secret things are probably going on right now. But what cognitive and psychological factors lead people into believing conspiracies with little or no evidence? Quite a few.

Let's look at the big picture first: a need for cognitive closure. Our brains are designed to seek answers, especially when faced with a big event that's produced a strong emotional response. If you wake in the night to the sound of a huge explosion that rattles the windows and shakes the floor, you want to know what caused it. You *need* to know what caused it—for a very simple reason: The ancient parts of your brain involved with survival have perceived it as a threat and need an explanation so they can prepare for it.

In the absence of an official answer, such as through trusted authorities or the media, you'll gravitate toward anything that supplies an answer. For some people, one of the appeals of religion is it supplies answers to questions big and small. Others might turn primarily to science, while still others will turn to any source with an answer that fits their beliefs.

So why do some people reject answers from authorities or the mass media? As you might have guessed already, the keyword is "trusted" authority and media. If you distrust a source, you'll be inclined to distrust their answers.

Conspiracies don't simply fill an emotional need to have answers to an important question; they fill the need for our overarching beliefs to be correct. Therefore, we'll choose any answer that fits and reinforces our beliefs and our trust in our sources of information. Keep this in mind later when we talk about QAnon.

Conspiracies can help organize world events in ways that fit our beliefs. They can also help explain previously unexplained phenomena (or offer a more satisfying explanation) as well as give us a sense of superiority. If we perceive we're seeing through a deception that no one else sees through, it makes us feel smarter, less prone to being manipulated, and, therefore, in many ways, superior to the masses who can't see through the deception.

Hopefully, you have a question right now. The need for cognitive closure and the need for an emotionally satisfying answer applies to almost everyone, but not everyone turns to conspiracy theories for answers to their questions. So what makes them unique? An interaction of cognitive traits.

When I teach the psychology of deception, my very first section is self-deception. The sad reality is that we lie to ourselves more than we lie to anyone else. Cognitive biases fuel this, but the greatest culprit is confirmation bias, in which we seek out information that specifically supports our beliefs, and we more readily encode any incoming information that supports our beliefs while disregarding anything that doesn't.

For example, if there's growing evidence your partner is cheating on you, but you have a deep-seated emotional need to believe the partner is faithful and that you aren't the kind of person who'd fall for a cheater, you're highly motivated to disregard the evidence. If I believe my political party only does good things and anything bad is because of the other party, I'll cling to evidence of the good my party does and dismiss or diminish the bad while exaggerating the bad by the other party and dismissing or diminishing the good.

Our brains use a lot of cognitive resources in defending our beliefs from countering information, and the more important a belief is to our worldview and self-perception, the more energy our brains will use to defend the belief.

This brings us to schema. A *schema* is a template or a way of understanding specific parts of our world so we can navigate our day-to-day lives. We develop schemas through experience and through early socialization.

A common example of schema is the "fast food schema," meaning our understanding of what a fast-food restaurant is and what kinds of food we can expect to receive there. Obviously, you learn to recognize the national chains, but you could drive through any small town and instantly recognize the local fast-food place. You'd know what kinds of food you might get there and the process of ordering it. You'd know it's not a fancy sit-down restaurant where you can expect a steak and a bottle of wine. You learn these things through experience.

How does this relate to conspiracy theory? If your world schema includes the idea that corruption exists at high levels, based on either government position or wealth, you're more likely to accept the idea that something secret is being done and covered up. The same acceptance occurs if you believe there are people of power who have the capability to carry out secret operations undetected and have access to technology beyond what's currently known to the general public. Your view of the world sets the stage for your belief in a conspiracy theory.

I'm often asked about the role of delusional disorder. It would be very easy for someone who fits the clinical criteria for delusional disorder to believe in conspiracies, but such a clinical condition isn't necessary. Indeed, throughout this book, I'll put greater emphasis on how people who'd otherwise be considered rational and "normal" can come to believe in sometimes outlandish and irrational conspiracies.

Why are we so motivated to brush off conspiracy theorists as delusional? A simple self-protective response: It makes us feel like we wouldn't fall for the same thing—that we'd be able to see through it. We'll address the specifics of this influence in several later chapters.

This sounds like fun theorizing, but has belief in conspiracy theory been studied empirically? Yes. Most of the studies fall across similar categories, so I'll grab a couple examples that cover the foundation. Viren Swami, Tomas Chamorro-Premuzic, and Adrian Furnham have conducted multiple studies on conspiracy theory beliefs. In 2010, they published the article "Unanswered Questions: A Preliminary Investigation of Personality and Individual Difference Predictors of 9/11 Conspiracist Beliefs" in *Applied Cognitive Psychology*. In this report, they discovered that beliefs specifically in 9/11 conspiracies correlated to beliefs in other conspiracies. Believers rated very high in political cynicism and defiance of authority, and they rated low in the "Big Five" measure of "agreeableness" but high in "openness."

What are the "Big Five" measures? They're personality traits of five spectrums within personality studies:

- *Conscientiousness:* organized, careful, and disciplined versus disorganized, careless, and impulsive
- *Neuroticism/emotional stability:* calm and secure versus anxious and insecure
- *Extraversion:* sociable versus reserved
- *Agreeableness:* trusting and helpful versus suspicious and uncooperative
- *Openness:* imaginative and independent versus practical and conforming

Belief in conspiracy theories correlated to greater suspiciousness and more imaginative thinking. If you study conspiracy beliefs, this shouldn't come as a big surprise.

In 2011, Hannah Darwin, Nick Neave, and Joni Holmes published the article "Belief in Conspiracy Theories. The Role of Paranormal Belief, Paranoid Ideation, and Schizotypy" in *Personality and Individual Differences*. This article went in the other direction, looking at cognitive dysfunctions found in some people who believed in conspiracy theories. They found high degrees of paranormal belief (especially processes that are currently thought to be scientifically impossible), paranoid ideation (hostile intent of powerful external agents), and correlations to symptoms of schizotypy, such as suspicion, magical thinking, odd beliefs, and social anxiety.

But again, I want to emphasize that in this book, I'm focusing on people who believe in conspiracies yet are thought to be otherwise rational-thinking people.

As we launch into the individual conspiracies, remember the anchors of the project management approach:

- Who's supposedly running the conspiracy?
- What's their goal?
- Does the goal make practical sense? Does it benefit those espousing the conspiracy?
- Does the method make practical sense? Is it the best method you could think of to achieve the goal with the greatest chance of success?
- How many people would it take to carry it out? The more people, the less likely it can succeed.
- Do you need to fake public records to carry it out? How many records and how long would it take?
- Does the method require "crisis actors" to publicly appear as victims of the event? How will you make sure they forever play that role and stay silent about the conspiracy?

Finally, why does our brain sometimes use fictional information when interpreting real-world events? It's partly a by-product of how fast the brain accesses stored information but fails to pay attention to the original source. The problem is compounded because our brain isn't well designed for processing media, especially fictional media. It wants to assume everything being processed is happening in our immediate environment. For example, I could spend Sunday afternoon crashed on the sofa watching a horror movie in which little blond children become possessed and start killing people. Consciously, I know it's just a movie; it's not really happening. But the deeper areas of my brain that handle emotional processing think all the information getting to them is happening in my immediate environment and will proceed to produce an emotional reaction. That's why movies can make us laugh, cry, or get scared even though we know the movie isn't real.

While I'm watching a horror movie, the higher-level processing of the frontal lobes keeps me from jumping off the sofa and running out of the house screaming in terror, but the emotional processing areas still generate an echo of the emotion. Additionally, my brain is storing the memory of the movie. All good so far. Then Monday morning, I'm leaving for campus, and when I open my front door, I see three blond children on the sidewalk in front of my house, and as I step outside, they pause and look at me. My brain immediately cues up the memory of that movie and gives me a fear response. My brain has just used fiction to interpret a real-world event.

In the 1960s, researcher George Gerbner found that people who watch a lot of crime-related TV rated their local crime rate as being higher than people who didn't watch as much of this type of TV. When asked about crime, their brains generated a feeling about the crime rate based on their personal experience with crime and part of that "personal" experience was through fictionalized crime on TV. To use a social media example: The brain searched the hashtag "crime" but didn't notice the additional hashtag "fiction" on much of what it recalled. Gerbner referred to this as the "cultivation effect" and later, with Larry Gross, expanded it to "cultivation theory." In a nutshell, media gets stored in our brains and we can be influenced by it later when interpreting the real world.

How does this apply to what we've been discussing? In action movies and spy films, the villain is often either a government carrying out secret operations or a mega-wealthy individual bent on taking over the world (or at least a big financial chunk of it). These fictional stories get stored in our memories and serve to reinforce suspicions of the real-world counterparts to those villains.

Few of us have any personal experience with a government carrying out a secret plan or a billionaire trying to take over the world. Our stored memories of these things come from the media. When news stories report government conspiracies being covered up or wealthy people being charged with crimes, it helps reinforce the fictional information we've already stored.

I'll bring in cultivation effect several times in later chapters to explain how interpretations of reality can be easily influenced by exposure to fictional media.

With these things in mind, let's dig into some common and popular conspiracy theories.

CHAPTER 3

CHEMTRAILS

We start with the granddaddy of modern conspiracy theories and one of the easiest to debunk: chemtrails.

What do conspiracy theorists claim they are? Cloudy trails of chemicals left at high altitudes by aircraft. What are they for? Well, here's where things get wild and wacky. Claims include mind-control drugs, poisons to kill people for the purpose of population control, forced vaccination, weather modification, general chemical or biological warfare, or any form of psychological manipulation.

As we go through the conspiracies in this book, we'll come across many single events or phenomena that have multiple conspiracy theories connected to them and we'll look at the viability of each conspiracy on its own. However, in the case of chemtrails, we can apply the project management approach to the method itself, and with just a few exceptions, we can challenge the validity of the phenomena regardless of the goal.

But first, we look at the official account of what's creating those cloudy streaks in the sky: condensation trails, better known as "vapor trails."

The effect is created when hot, humid air from an engine encounters cold surrounding air at high altitudes, forming tiny ice crystals, which appear as visible clouds. Variations in atmospheric pressure and humidity dictate whether vapor trails will form and for how long they'll stay visible. The greater the atmospheric saturation, the longer the trails will remain. High-altitude winds will further determine the spread of the trail—sometimes stretching out to form sheets of cirrus-like clouds. There can be extreme variations by altitude, meaning planes that seem to be crossing the same space can form different trails or one forms a trail and one doesn't. There can even be variations by the type of plane and type of engine.

The science behind vapor trail formation is why we're covering this conspiracy theory first. Many of the conspiracies later in this book are fueled by a lack of scientific knowledge or understanding, and when we don't understand something, we'll fill the gaps with whatever explanation is suggested. This is another case of a need for cognitive closure. Failing to understand physics fuels these conspiracies and is a big component later in understanding why people believe the collapse of the Twin Towers looked like a controlled demolition.

Are there precedents in our personal experiences to set the stage for the belief that vapor trails are chemical trails? Yes. Planes dusting crops, spraying pesticides over farmland, dropping flame retardant over wildfires, experimenting with cloud seeding, and releasing smoke while performing at airshows. We've either seen these images personally or through the media, so they provide a foundation for the belief that vapor trails aren't simply ice crystals.

But those precise experiences also drive the first nail in the coffin of the chemtrail conspiracy. In what way do the clouds of chemicals produced by crop dusters, or cloud seeders, or fire-retardant planes (or even planes simply dropping water on fires) look different from vapor trails? They immediately drift downward. There's little or no horizontal spread and no vertical spread. They move only downward, while vapor trails spread in every direction.

Another problem would be the expectation that anything sprayed from more than 30,000 feet would get to the ground or be able to target a specific location. At that altitude, there'd be very little, if any, control over where it went or in what concentrations it would sustain when it finally reached the ground.

Applying these considerations to the project management approach produces some other problems.

If the goal is to expose the population to a chemical for whatever reason, is spraying it at high altitude the best way to deliver it? You'll be covering literally millions of acres of empty land, hoping dissipated remnants reach your target. For the chemical to have the desired effect in such a small dose, it would have to be tremendously toxic in its concentrated form in the tanks. If planes are spraying it, there must be nozzles on the plane to release the chemicals and those would have the concentrated form of the chemical on them, which means you'd need servicepeople in hazmat suits at the airports to clean them. That increases the number of people who must know about it.

If commercial airlines are spraying it, the pilots need to know about it and the airplane manufacturers would know about it, so you're already creating a population of conspirators that goes far beyond what's reasonable if you expect it to remain a secret.

If those aren't commercial airliners spreading it— as some claim—but secret military or government aircraft instead, then they're flying along commercial routes and just happen to time perfectly with scheduled commercial flights, which means the commercial flights are fake. So the airlines have to be aware of it. The airports are putting it on the schedule even though there are no planes at the gates, so they have to be in on it too. Again, it's too many people, especially relatively low-paid people in jobs with frequent turnover, to expect it would stay secret and no one would ever reveal it.

But here's the biggest problem: If you're in the secret Illuminati, Deep State, black ops government group tasked with exposing the general public to this chemical, is this really the best plan you could come up with to do this? Spray it into the air where everyone can see it? And if this is the plan you choose, are you going to do it in clear daylight? No. You'd do it on cloudy days or at night—when it's not so obvious.

Are there better ways to deliver such a chemical without the need for it to be so concentrated and toxic and still get it to as many people as possible? My classes come up with these as their first choices: food additives and drinking water. Given the complexity of the open-air plan and all the people it would involve, it would be much easier to have a shadow-operated facility that produces "preservatives" and inserts them into nearly all prepackaged foods. Government "water-quality testing" could easily include the insertion of the chemical. Even the testing of rural wells could include contamination with the chemical and involve fewer people and be less obvious than the "spray it in the air" plan.

What about the idea that it's a method for controlling climate? There's a nugget of truth to that one, but it doesn't require secretly spraying chemicals into the air. Climate control is already proven to occur from the dissipation of lingering vapor trails as they spread, combine, and turn into sheets of cirrus-like clouds.

Proven? How could something like that be proven? It would be unlikely that an empirical, controlled attempt to change weather would be approved given the uncertainty of what might happen. But real-world events sometimes give us the opportunity to study effects we could never otherwise ethically attempt. The three-day grounding of all commercial aircraft in the United States after the 9/11 attacks provided such an opportunity. The initial evidence came from anecdotal observations by people in highly populated areas where dense commercial air traffic was common. They noticed the sky appeared unusually clear compared with most days and that the blue was a more vivid blue. Was this because of the lack of spreading vapor trails from aircraft?

It didn't take long for scientists to start collecting weather data from the days before, during, and after the grounding of aircraft and comparing the data. David J. Travis, Andrew M. Carleton, and Ryan G. Lauritsen from the University of Wisconsin at Whitewater took it a step further and collected data from about 4,000 weather stations in the continental United States spanning the years 1971 to 2000 and compared that with the 2001 data around the time of the air traffic grounding. They found that the grounding increased the average temperature range by about two degrees Celsius. Obviously, this would vary by region depending on air traffic density and average atmospheric moisture.

The point is, there's valid scientific evidence that humans can potentially create mild changes in weather. As we'll see in several later conspiracy theories, pieces of legitimate science are often used to support claims that stretch the science beyond reality. Yes, we could influence temperature but only regionally and just by a few degrees. There's no evidence we can do things like create and direct hurricanes, cause tornadoes, or bring disastrous winter weather to specific regions of the country. None of these findings create a foundation for a secret government weather machine in Alaska, Area 51, or anywhere else.

You'll also notice another trend in these conspiracies: They don't involve secret operations to produce positive results that would help the general population. Quite the opposite. The claims usually involve the government or some cabal of the wealthy and powerful wanting to hurt a large number of people.

There's a logic flaw with this assumption: Where do the wealthy and powerful get their wealth and power? They mostly extract it from the labor of the masses. The last thing they'd want to do is drastically decrease the population of the people they rely on for their wealth. We'll address this point several times in later chapters.

What about mind control? Are chemtrails spraying mind-control drugs over the entire population to cloud their minds to the reality of what's going on around them or make them more susceptible to manipulation? You might have seen this flaw yourself: Why are the conspiracy theorists not affected by it? What allows them to see through it if they're exposed to the same chemicals as everyone else?

What about making people sick so they'll require treatment from Big Pharma to treat these illnesses? Unfortunately for this theory, there's no disease—not even the COVID-19 pandemic—large enough to be explained by chemical agents being spread to the entire population. The rates would be extraordinary. As you can imagine, there are many conspiracies circulating about the COVID-19 pandemic and vaccine. We'll address those in Chapter 10.

To summarize the project management approach to chemtrails, we identified multiple issues:

- Spraying in the open air on clear days is too obvious.
- It would take too many people to carry it out—far more people than could be expected to keep it quiet.

- It wouldn't effectively achieve the goal regardless of which specific goal we're considering.
- It's not the best plan you could devise for achieving the goal. There are many other possibilities that are simpler, involve fewer people, and have a better chance of achieving the goal.

Remember Occam's razor: The simplest plan is usually the best one. This principle is a primary driver for where we place conspiracies on the conspiracy theory spectrum—from likely to unlikely or rational to irrational. Chemtrails fall well on the unlikely, irrational side of the spectrum.

But there's another reason I bring up Occam's razor now. You might think this book is entirely about tearing down conspiracy theories. It's more about understanding where a conspiracy falls on the spectrum and being able to critically think about whether specific conspiracies are rational. In Chapter 4, we'll cover a famous conspiracy theory that has many variations that fall on the probable and realistic side of the spectrum: the Kennedy assassination.

CHAPTER 4

THE KENNEDY ASSASSINATION

If chemtrails is the granddaddy of modern conspiracies, the Kennedy assassination is the father. Only the September 11, 2001, attacks on the United States have produced more conspiracy theories and no other event has seen its conspiracy theories traverse such a wide range of media—from articles to books to full-length documentaries. The lack of full release of all the documents related to the investigations keeps this topic alive more than half a century after the event. In 2018, the Trump administration cited national security interests as a reason for delaying the release of more documents, and in 2021, the Biden administration claimed administrative delays because of COVID-related staffing shortages and work backlogs as a reason for further delays. It's no surprise that conspiracies would continue to be fueled by such delays more than 50 years later.

Conspiracies in this chapter range from foreign sources, such as Cuba and the Soviet Union, to domestic suspects, including Vice President Lyndon B. Johnson and future president George H.W. Bush. It seems that over the years, no one is immune from being tied to this conspiracy in one way or another. In the 2016 presidential race, then-candidate Donald Trump revived a conspiracy connecting the father of Texas senator Ted Cruz to the assassination.

We'll repeat this point many times later when we discuss certain conspiracies being on the "rational and probable" side of the conspiracy spectrum. We're not endorsing them or saying they're true; we're simply saying they pass many or all of our criteria for an operation that could realistically be carried out and could effectively achieve a goal. They're expected and rational methods someone trying to achieve a specific goal might choose. There are some aspects of specific conspiracy theories around the Kennedy assassination that don't quite meet these criteria and we'll discuss those specific points as we come to them.

But first, as I'll do in each chapter, here's the official record of what happened. In late November 1963, President Kennedy was scheduled for a two-day swing through Texas, including stops in San Antonio, Houston, and Fort Worth (on November 21st) as well as Dallas, Austin, and Johnson City (on November 22nd).

On the morning of November 22nd, the president and first lady gave speeches at a breakfast in Fort Worth. Then they departed for Dallas, where they arrived at Dallas Love Field Airport in northwest Dallas at 11:38 a.m. local time. A waiting motorcade was to take them from the airport, through downtown, and to the Dallas Trade Mart.

We need to pause here for a moment to address one conspiracy claim that has long been proven untrue: That the route was changed at the last minute. It wasn't. The route had been published locally prior to their arrival to give citizens a chance to see the president as he passed through town. This is why there were dozens of people along the road with still and motion cameras. Keep in mind, this was in the days prior to cell phones with cameras. It wasn't typical for the average citizen to be carrying cameras around with them during the day and just happen to catch the president on an unannounced route.

There were more than 20 vehicles in the motorcade, with the president's car—the SS-100-X, a 1961 Lincoln Continental specifically modified to be a presidential limousine—the second in line. (These modifications are going to be important later when considering several of the proposed conspiracies.) At 12:29 p.m., the motorcade entered Dealey Plaza. At 12:30 p.m., they turned onto Elm Street. Shortly thereafter, three shots rang out. One struck President Kennedy in the back of the neck and exited through his throat. Another shot struck his head, explosively damaging his skull. Governor John Connally, riding in the seat in front of Kennedy, was wounded by at least one of the same bullets that passed through the president.

According to the official report from the Warren Commission, the shots were fired from the sixth-floor window at the southeast corner of the Texas School Book Depository by Lee Harvey Oswald. A total of three shots were fired: Two bullets struck the president and one missed.

After killing the president, Oswald fled the area, briefly returned to his rooming house, but then quickly departed. At 12:45 p.m., he was spotted in the Oak Cliff area by officer J.D. Tippit, who was patrolling the area as part of the search zone for a suspect in the shooting of the president. He stopped Oswald, who fit the description. Oswald shot him five times, killing him, then fled. Oswald briefly hid inside a Hardy Shoe Store to avoid police cars driving past, then ducked into the Texas Theater without purchasing a ticket. The theater's cashier notified police and Oswald was apprehended a short time later.

Oswald wasn't immediately identified as the person who assassinated the president. He was identified by witnesses who saw him shoot Officer Tippit and then flee. Oswald denied he'd shot the officer. At approximately 1 a.m. on November 23rd, he was formally charged with assassinating the president. On the morning of November 24th, while being transferred from the Dallas City Jail to the Dallas County Jail, he was shot and killed by local nightclub owner Jack Ruby, who was arrested on the scene. The shooting of Oswald was captured on camera and on live TV.

Because Oswald initially claimed innocence and was then killed, we can't know his story in his own words. There's no confession to specify motive. Everything regarding him is superficial and comes from outside investigation.

Conspiracy theories exploded almost immediately after the Kennedy assassination. The general public felt that either the Soviet Union or Cuba was behind it, Oswald didn't act alone, or there was some attempt at covering up information. Part of this was fueled by eyewitness accounts that conflicted with some of the official stories. Eyewitnesses claimed to hear multiple shots, to hear shots from directions other than the Book Depository, and to have seen suspicious people in various places near street level, especially the famous grassy knoll.

A side note here: Many conspiracies are born when early eyewitness accounts don't match later reports. The problem with this is that initial eyewitness reports, even early media reports, are frequently wrong, but conspiracy theorists decide initial reports must be true and any later report that doesn't match is an attempt at a cover-up. We'll run into this again when we cover the 9/11 conspiracies in Chapter 7.

To try to control the brushfire of conspiracies, President Johnson issued Executive Order 11130 on November 29, 1963, which was later authorized by Senate Joint Resolution 137 to appoint a commission to investigate and report on the assassination of the president. It came to be known as the Warren Commission, named after its chairman, Chief Justice Earl Warren. There were a total of seven members of the commission—all well known and well regarded at the time, including one name you might recognize: future president Gerald R. Ford.

On September 24, 1964, the commission released its 888-page report stating Oswald had acted alone, he fired three shots, and Ruby had acted alone when he killed Oswald. Case closed? Obviously not. Once you have suspicions of high-level cover-ups, nothing is going to convince people otherwise. It wasn't until later that the public learned the CIA withheld some information from the commission, especially information related to Cuba. It's not hard to imagine how that opened the door for a parade of conspiracy theories. Before we start addressing specific conspiracies, we'll take the official story to see how it stands up with our project management approach. Does it make sense?

It does. Oswald had anti-government leanings, he worked at the Book Depository building for a month, and the president's motorcade was going to drive directly past the building. There'd be easy opportunity from an upper-floor window. Does the plan achieve the goal of killing the president? Yes. Would it involve very many people who'd need to keep it secret? No. In fact, only one: himself. Is there a better plan you could come up with that would have a greater chance of success? Debatable. It's hard to imagine a better setup than the sixth floor of the building because you're away from people who could stop you or get a clear look at you and it gives you more time to escape afterward. This last point is what raises questions about the idea of other shooters by the grassy knoll or, for that matter, anywhere at street level. The presence, number, and movement of citizens at street level would've been very unpredictable and on paper would seem to make escape nearly impossible, while the presence and movement of people on the sixth floor of the Book Depository building would've been much more predictable. From a project management perspective, it's a perfect plan—almost a perfect storm of pieces all falling together at the right time to set up the opportunity.

That's why so many conspiracy theories formed around the event. It seems almost too perfect, too coincidental that this person would just happen to be in the perfect place and the route would just happen to go past a perfect spot for an assassination attempt without the Secret Service noticing the problem and taking steps to address it ahead of time. And even more unsettling is the idea that a single disgruntled citizen could take down the leader of the free world. It *had* to be something more complex than that, right?

Keep something in mind when it comes to theories critical of the Secret Service: The Kennedy assassination led to changes in many of the security procedures used by the Secret Service today. Later, the assassination attempt on Ronald Reagan produced even more changes. At the time of the Kennedy assassination, only three presidents had ever been assassinated: Abraham Lincoln in 1865, James Garfield in 1881, and William McKinley in 1901. There had been attempts on Theodore Roosevelt (after he'd left office but was running for a third term), Franklin D. Roosevelt, and Harry Truman—but none succeeded. There was great confidence that security could adequately protect the president. An identical appearance and motorcade route by a president today would result in much different security procedures, which would prevent a similar attempt. It's always important to consider the environment of the time.

There have been entire conspiracy documentaries and books produced on this event—far more than what I could address here—but most of them fall on the rational end of the conspiracy spectrum. However, a few of them have some weaknesses, so let us look at some of the broader conspiracies and where they might be faulty.

We must start with the umbrella conspiracy that covers them all: Lee Harvey Oswald either didn't act alone or was involved with some other group interested in killing the president. These range from Oswald being an active participant in the planning to him simply being set up as the fall guy for a group wishing to remain secret.

In the weeks after the shooting, everything Oswald owned was taken as evidence and pretty much everyone who knew him was interviewed extensively to determine his motive. This is where conspiracy theorists tend to cherry-pick the information to support their specific views. If information seems to support Oswald as the lone gunman with no other affiliation, it gets rejected by conspiracists as an attempt by the Warren Commission to support their official report, whereas if the same sources of information seem to support the theory that Oswald was part of a greater conspiracy, conspiracists will fully embrace the information.

For example, while being investigated after the shooting, Oswald became a suspect in the attempted assassination of retired US major general Edwin Walker in Dallas on April 10, 1963. Oswald allegedly fired through a window into Walker's home, resulting in a mild wound to his forearm. This was used as evidence to support the claim that Oswald was a rogue and likely to go after a person of authority if he had the opportunity.

Oswald also attempted to defect to the Soviet Union during a trip to that country in October 1959, but he was denied and forced to leave the country. This is often used as evidence he was part of a Soviet plan to kill the president.

There are procedural and logic problems in any conspiracy that has Oswald as part of a larger coordinated plan. We'll address these as we discuss the plans individually, but first I want to address the claim that Oswald was simply set up as the fall guy and took no part in the actual shooting (and by some claims wasn't even present).

How does this fit our criteria for a good cover-up? Poorly. His history would make him too risky as a loose end for such a setup. Other theories claim he was too poor of a marksman to be able to carry out the task. This would also make him undesirable as a scapegoat for the plan. You'd want someone who investigators would consider a viable person to carry out the plan—at least on the surface.

Here's an alternative that would make more sense: Oswald is brought in on the plan, other people are going to be the shooters, and you have him there thinking he'll be a shooter or thinking he'll aid in the getaway after the shooting. Once the shooting is complete, you terminate him before the police have a chance to apprehend him and you plant evidence to make it seem he was a lone wolf shooter. End of story. Achieves the goal and involves very few people.

There's another popular point we need to debunk before we move on to specific conspiracies: the "magic bullet"—the idea it was impossible for a shot fired from Oswald on the sixth floor of the Book Depository to hit Kennedy and Governor Connally without doing some fancy gymnastics in the process. A key error helped perpetuate this: the idea that Kennedy and Connally were sitting at equal elevations within the car. You'll find many diagrams online that claim the official trajectory of the bullets was impossible from the sixth floor of the Book Depository given the level position of the two men. Remember, Kennedy's car wasn't a standard 1961 Lincoln Continental; it was the modified SS-100-X, specifically designed to be the presidential limousine. Part of this modification was a hydraulic rear seat that could be elevated to give the public a better view of the person riding in the back. If you look carefully at pictures from the moments before the assassination, you'll notice Kennedy is sitting several inches higher than Connally and is leaning more toward the outside of the car as he waves at the crowd. Given this positioning, the trajectory perfectly fits a shot coming from above.

With these in mind, let's look at several conspiracy theories centering around the idea that Oswald was involved with other groups or individuals who in some way helped him carry out the shooting.

Vice President Lyndon B. Johnson

Johnson would benefit from the death of the president, given that it would make him president. The motive is there. Additionally, there are verified accounts Kennedy intended to replace Johnson on the ticket in the 1964 presidential election. Would that be enough to plan an assassination? Was the presidency that important to Johnson? It doesn't seem so, given that after winning re-election in 1964, Johnson chose not to run again in 1968. Also, the assassination seemed like an open-and-shut case solely convicting Oswald. Why would Johnson risk such an extensive investigation by opening the Warren Commission? What would be the consequences if discovered? Likely the death penalty for treason and a forever tarnished history. This is one we can quite safely put on the unlikely side of the spectrum.

The Soviet Union and Cuba

I put these two together because the failed Bay of Pigs Invasion in 1961 (in which Cuban rebels trained and assisted by the United States intended to take down Cuban leader Fidel Castro) and the 1962 Cuban Missile Crisis (in which the US Navy blockaded Soviet ships from delivering materials for nuclear missile launch platforms in Cuba) give the Soviet Union and Cuba tremendous motivation in wanting to eliminate the US president—and the Warren Commission dug deep into both possibilities during their investigation. As I mentioned earlier, it was the failure of the CIA to fully disclose intelligence related to Cuba, including the later-revealed Operation Northwoods, that further fueled conspiracy theories around the assassination and the validity of the Warren Commission findings.

Where would the Soviet Union and Cuba fall on our conspiracy spectrum? On the rational side—with a few caveats. Was it possible in 1963 for a foreign government to plan and carry out the assassination of a president? Yes. In fact, given the number of people on the street watching Kennedy, many of them much closer than Oswald, any of a dozen of people could have taken shots at the president if there was no intention of the shooter escaping.

Would it have been practical for a foreign government to make the attempt? Not really. We run into the issue of potential consequences if the plan failed, especially consequences to Cuba because the US government was actively looking for any reason to take out Fidel Castro. Another reason it wouldn't be practical is US presidents run for election every four years and Kennedy was only a year away from another election. Would it be worth the risk? And realistically, would Johnson's approach to Cuba and the Soviet Union have been that much different?

Oswald had attempted to defect to the Soviet Union years earlier and had been denied. Many point to this as a possible connection between Oswald and the Soviets, but by the same token, a foreign power plotting an assassination would be unlikely to solicit the help of someone like Oswald. His history would make him very high risk. But his history also creates a merry-go-round of conspiracy justification. Oswald wouldn't be a good choice to help with your plan, but at the same time, he might be the perfect choice to help with your plan because his history would make it seem obvious he was a lone wolf assassin.

So we turn to the project management approach. You work at a high level in Soviet intelligence and your group has been given the task of assassinating the US president. The Cuban Missile Crisis was an embarrassment for your country, so motivation is there to send a message—not just to the United States but to the next person to hold that office. You have access to records of US citizens who've defected to the Soviet Union as well as others, such as Oswald, who wanted to but were denied. You have people within the United States providing intelligence. You have access to sharpshooters who could easily carry out the task. Using a US citizen, no matter how friendly they are to your cause, is a loose end and a potential risk for the plan to fail or be discovered. Would this be a viable plan and would Kennedy's visit to Dallas be the best option? Not at all. In mere months, the 1964 presidential campaign would begin and Kennedy would be making multiple public appearances— some planned well in advance—that would provide multiple, better opportunities.

Side note: Did the Soviet Union really deny Oswald's request to defect? Or was that a cover story to hide his agreement to act as a domestic agent for the Soviet Union on US soil for whatever operation they might need him to carry out? This is very unlikely, if not impossible, because it would've never become public record that Oswald had sought to defect. He'd simply have been a visitor who went home, with nothing to draw the interest of US intelligence. This was, after all, the height of the Cold War and international paranoia in intelligence communities was high. Similarly, Oswald's trip to Mexico City the weeks before the assassination, when he supposedly went to the Cuban and

Soviet embassies seeking to defect but was again denied, would've been covered up if he were a pawn set up by either of those countries.

If the Warren Commission had found evidence of involvement by either Cuba or the Soviet Union, would they have been motivated to hide it? In the case of Cuba, not at all. As we mentioned earlier, the United States was looking for any reason to invade Cuba and take out Castro. Attaching him to the assassination of the president would've been a gift on a silver platter. But what about the Soviet Union? That's a bigger dog with much greater consequences. The world had walked the edge of nuclear war during the Cuban Missile Crisis and connecting the assassination of the president to that nation would've put us right back on, or maybe over, the brink of war.

A question might have just occurred to you: With so many accusations of secret plans, fake documents, and people being set up or framed for things they didn't do, why would such powerful forces pass up the opportunity to fake evidence, point the finger at Cuba, and finally send the military in to take out Fidel Castro? That's a valid question. It was the perfect opportunity. Perhaps such national and international conspiracy isn't as common as we think?

These problems aside, assassination conspiracies involving other nations still fall on the possible and rational side of our spectrum because they'd require no leap of logic to imagine the motivation and the nations would have the ability to carry them out if they wanted.

Organized Crime

This one is popular because President Kennedy's brother, Robert F. Kennedy, then attorney general, actively sought the prosecution of crime bosses—and Jack Ruby, who killed Oswald, was thought to have ties to organized crime. Again, the Warren Commission determined there was no evidence connecting organized crime to the assassinations of either Kennedy or Oswald, but that didn't stop people from wondering. Supposedly, the CIA had approached at least one known crime boss about carrying out an attempted assassination of Fidel Castro (again, a Cuba connection).

This one comes down to a central root: The mob hired Oswald, who was supposed to escape, but because he got captured, Jack Ruby killed him so he couldn't talk.

Problem number one: Oswald did talk prior to being killed. He simply didn't confess anything and it makes no practical sense that you'd kill Oswald in such a public way in a place where you'd be immediately apprehended. Again, a group with high-level connections should easily be able to get rid of Oswald at a different time when he's more isolated, such as in a jail cell.

This is another one that's possible and rational, the motivation is there, but aspects of it don't make sense. If the anger is directed at Robert Kennedy, why target the president? The attorney general would be an easier target and send the same message. Taking out the president invites an unprecedented wrath if the plan is exposed.

George H.W. Bush

Future director of the CIA, future vice president, and later president. This one is interesting because it ties to current conspiracies about why some documents associated with the investigation still haven't been released. Although George H.W. Bush is no longer alive, his son George W. still is. Some believe that's a reason the family connection to the assassination is still being protected to this day. This is an easy one to dismiss. It came out years after the fact, mostly because Bush happened to be in Dallas the day before the assassination and flew to Tyler, Texas, the day of the assassination. A CIA memo claimed a "George Bush" was briefed just days after the assassination. George H.W. Bush wasn't director of the CIA until 1976. In 1963, he was preparing for a Senate run. Why is this one easy to discard? No motive, no obvious connections to make it happen, and no benefit from it happening. This one is simply a case of conspiracy theorists finding some loose associations and attempting to tie them together into something significant.

There were many other less supported and less popular conspiracies around Kennedy—everything from the Federal Reserve to aliens. (Yes, Kennedy was supposedly going to expose the existence of aliens and a treaty Eisenhower had signed with them.) Take your pick.

Overall, except for aliens, we put most of the conspiracies on the possible and mostly rational side of the spectrum, but there's a key reason we must be skeptical with all of them: John F. Kennedy was the president of the United States. You'd need reams of paper to list all the people who might want to kill a president. It can be very reassuring to think there had to be some powerful group playing out a grand conspiracy to pull off the assassination of a president rather than think a single citizen was able to pull it off.

Most realistically? Maybe Oswald really did want to defect to a Communist country, and after additional rejections in Mexico City, he thought killing the president would make him a hero in those countries. But most of the evidence points toward a single individual who just happened to have the opportunity and managed to do it. Maybe the as-yet-unreleased documents will one day shine a light on new evidence, but for now, the Warren Commission seems to have come to the best conclusion they could reach given the information they had.

CHAPTER 5

THE MOON LANDING HOAX

The Apollo program began in 1961 as a planned continuation of the Mercury and Gemini space programs, with the purpose of putting humans on the moon. The first crewed flight was conducted in October 1968 (*Apollo* 7), and just two months later, *Apollo 8* (with no landing module) orbited the moon for the first time.

In March 1969, *Apollo 9* was the first flight of the complete spacecraft, including command module, service module, and lunar module, but it stayed in Earth's orbit so all systems and procedures could be tested. Just two months later, *Apollo 10* took the full spacecraft to the moon but didn't land. They served as a "dress rehearsal" testing all procedures and systems for the following *Apollo 11* mission, which landed on the moon on July 20, 1969. Six more missions followed over the next two years—all but one (*Apollo 13*) landing on the moon. The program was inevitably shut down because of budget cutbacks and, to be honest, lack of public interest in more moon missions.

Given the popularity of the moon hoax theory today, it might surprise you to hear that at the time of the Apollo program, very few people believed it was being faked. It's an important point to consider the time and place of an event as well as the cultural attitudes of the time when evaluating how conspiracies form and spread and what motivates them.

We already considered the public revelation of MK-Ultra (the government drug experiments) and its revelation of being related to Watergate. It's impossible to understate the impact of Watergate on the growing cultural awareness in the 1970s of the government's willingness and ability to carry out secret operations and the resulting increase in public suspicion of not just government but also any powerful group (real or imagined).

Suspicions around the validity of the Apollo program in general and the moon landings specifically exploded in the 1970s with the publication of Bill Kaysing's self-published book *We Never Went to the Moon* in 1976. No one cared that Kaysing didn't have the scientific or technical expertise to critique the program. He'd been a technical writer for Rocketdyne's jet propulsion laboratory and this was all the experience the general public needed. Some of his other works were scientific gems, such as *Land and How to Buy It for a Few Dollars an Acre*; *How to Eat Well on Less Than a Dollar a Day*; and *Fell's Beginner's Guide to Motorcycling*. Prior to writing his book on the moon landing, he'd left his job with Rocketdyne, rejected all external media, got rid of his TV, and cancelled his newspaper subscription. He moved his family into an RV to live a "year-long vacation" traveling, resulting in his family leaving him. He then lived a transient lifestyle until working his way back into writing and then publishing his own book.

His book set the foundation for many of the common themes in the moon landing conspiracies: We didn't have the technology to return from the moon, astronauts would die from radiation, there were no stars in the photos, there was no blast crater under the lunar lander, etc. We'll address these as we go.

But we'll start first with the project management approach to the conspiracy. If the goal is to make the general public believe the United States went to the moon without actually doing it, what's the best way to do it and, more importantly, why take the risk and attempt it in the first place? If it's scientifically impossible, then not only can the United States not do it, but neither can anyone else. So why fake it?

The most common response to the last question: to appease the public by fulfilling President Kennedy's challenge to put a man on the moon before the end of the decade. In addition to being a nod toward Kennedy, it would be a perceived foot up on the Soviet Union during the space race and help fuel the perception of US superiority over Communism at a time when the Cold War was publicly stagnant and the general public was burned out and not responding as powerfully to the Cold War propaganda of the 1950s.

Valid point. But within this point is also the single greatest reason the moon landing wasn't faked: The Soviet Union had the technology to verify that we went and would've been the first to expose it if we didn't. It would've been a global humiliation to the United States, an opportunity no international enemy would pass up, and especially tempting for the Soviet Union after being embarrassed years earlier during the Cuban Missile Crisis.

The moon landing conspiracies are a great example of how otherwise rational and logical people can be led to believe in conspiracy theories. The tactic is best displayed in the Fox TV special *Conspiracy Theory: Did We Land on the Moon?*, which first aired in 2001 and presented several of the "unexplained" details from the moon landing I'll cover in a moment.

What's the tactic? Present something as mysterious or unexplained when it does have an easy explanation, but don't present the explanation. Before the audience has a chance to think it through for themselves, move on to the next supposedly unexplained detail. For example, the pictures of the lunar lander show relatively undisturbed dust under the main engine. Shouldn't there be a blast crater there if the main engine was used on landing? Mysterious! The actual answer? The main engine was used for deceleration but wasn't used for the final descent to the surface. Smaller thrusters on the legs of the lander were used for the final touchdown. So no, there'd be no crater or disturbance directly beneath the lander.

What happens if I throw a series of "unexplained mysteries" at you in quick succession without letting you think about them rationally? You'll start to have the gut feeling that even if you don't usually believe in conspiracies, it's odd there are so many peculiar questions and you'll start to feel like something isn't right about the situation. Maybe there really was a faked landing and cover-up! You can see this tactic used frequently in any program attempting to present "unexplained mysteries."

Polls of the general public found that the Fox "documentary" had a measurable impact on the belief that there was something peculiar about the moon landing and that something just didn't add up.

In class, I've shown the original program to students, but instead of letting it play out uninterrupted, I'll pause after each "mystery" and explain why it's not mysterious at all. After doing this, the class is more likely to find the "documentary" manipulative rather than revealing.

As an aside, it seems rather counterintuitive that many "science" channels on cable today will air programs of such "mysteries." However, they can be great opportunities to practice critical thinking. If you can find some of these programs, watch for the tactic!

So what are the logical explanations for the supposed mysteries surrounding the moon landing? I'll start with the alleged problems with light and shadow in the pictures, which some people claim is evidence of multiple light sources. I clump these together because they all have the same root problem.

In moon photos in which you can see into the distance, conspiracy theorists have noted that the shadows of different objects don't align along the same plane. They appear at slightly different angles to each other. They claim this is a sign there was more than one light source when you'd expect the only light source to be the sun. A key problem with this theory is visual perspective. It's difficult to know the actual size, distance, and surface variations. Any of these factors could create what appeared to be differences in the angle of shadows from the view of the camera. How? Think about looking at an old railroad track from an angle. It might look like it's completely twisted and not parallel, but when you stand on the track and look down it straight on, you see it's straight. Why? Because the twisting you saw from an angle was vertical warping of the track, not horizontal warping—and from a distance, you couldn't tell.

The other picture most referenced is the astronaut descending from the lander. The lander is mostly in shadow, but the astronaut is clearly visible within the shadow. This is seen as evidence there was a separate light illuminating the astronaut. The easier answer? It's a contrast effect because of exposure. There's shadow on the lander, but the astronaut's light-colored suit is illuminated by the light reflected from the lunar surface. The shadow isn't as dark as it appears; it's darkened by the contrast produced from the bright lunar surface. The same camera effect is the reason you don't see stars in the sky in the images taken from the moon. The sunlight reflecting from the ground is producing too much light for the film to pick up the comparatively minor light produced by stars. This same effect is in practice when city lights dilute your view of stars in the sky at night. Take a drive out into the country away from city lights and notice the difference.

Think of it this way: If you're out on a sunny day and step into a shadow, do you disappear? No. But if someone standing in the sunlight takes your picture, you might not be visible at all—you're a dark blur. However, if you're wearing clothing brighter than your surroundings, you might stand out in the shadow because of the light reflecting from the sunlit ground outside the shadow.

There's a bigger problem with the claims of multiple light sources. If there were multiple light sources, there'd be multiple shadows on at least some of the objects. In none of the moon landing photos are there any hints of multiple shadows on any object. Therefore, the light effects are because of perspective and contrast.

Another common target is the picture of Buzz Aldrin taken by Neil Armstrong—a picture clear enough that if you zoom in on the reflection in Aldrin's helmet, you can see Armstrong in the near distance where he took the picture. So why is there no sign of Armstrong holding a camera? This one is kind of ridiculous because two conspiracy theories collide here. The astronauts didn't carry a camera in their hands; they had a camera mounted on the front of their suit. That's why Armstrong isn't seen *holding* a camera in the reflection.

The other related conspiracy acknowledges the suit-mounted cameras and claims the photos are too well done and too well centered to be taken from a suit-mounted camera. Why is this no issue at all? Two reasons: First, the astronauts received a lot of training on every aspect of the mission, including taking pictures with the cameras. Second, the pictures aren't *that* perfect. NASA cropped and centered original pictures before releasing them to the public so they'd look better. There's no mystery at all about the pictures themselves or the reflection in Aldrin's helmet.

Think of it another way: If Armstrong is in the perfect position in Aldrin's helmet reflection to have taken the picture but didn't take the picture, who did? Where's the camera that took the picture?

This chapter would be far too long if I addressed each piece of supposed evidence that the landing was fake—you can google the rest of it—but there's one last conspiracy I want to address because in many ways it contradicts itself: Filmmaker Stanley Kubrick filmed the fake footage of the landing on a secret soundstage. Why does this contradict itself? If someone believes in any of these other pieces of "evidence" that the landing was fake, then it's impossible Kubrick filmed it because a filmmaker of his caliber wouldn't make such obvious mistakes. He'd make it perfect. As some debunkers sarcastically say: "Kubrick agreed to film the footage, but because he's a perfectionist, he insisted it be shot on location on the moon."

Moon Hoax and Project Management

Aside from the issues with the supposed "evidence" of a hoax, how does the general idea of faking the moon landing fit into our criteria for a valid operation and cover-up?

Assuming the goal is to fool the general public and the world into thinking the United States put people on the moon—therefore fulfilling President Kennedy's challenge and establishing dominance over the Soviet Union in the space race—then it does achieve that goal.

Is the goal practical and reasonable? Not really. If it's scientifically impossible to send people to the moon—as some conspiracy theorists claim—then countries would simply admit it. Such an admission would mean no country could establish such dominance and further scientific advances would easily expose the lie. Aside from that, if the only technological challenge was putting people on the moon and returning them, dominance of space over the Soviet Union had already been achieved by sending people to orbit the moon and return to Earth.

Would it require very many people to carry off such a conspiracy? Yes—way too many to realistically believe such a plan could ever be carried out. This factor by itself places this conspiracy on the "irrational and impossible" end of our conspiracy spectrum. It simply couldn't be done.

Could we reduce the number of people who'd need to be in on it? If everyone involved with creating the technology and carrying out the mission knew it was impossible and was going to be faked, it would involve more than 400,000 people—in government and in hundreds of private industries. Imagine the money and fame any one of those people could get by being the one to provide the mass media with an exclusive story blowing up the entire charade.

But not everyone needs to know. Many of those people could think they were developing technology that had a chance to work. Let's try to pull it off. So who do we need? Obviously, the astronauts would be in on it and officials at NASA would know. And if you're building a soundstage and developing a fake moon scenario, then you also have people involved in that production. By itself, that would require hundreds of people. You're launching a massive Saturn V rocket on live TV with live crowds watching and the rocket itself visible from miles away, then later retrieving the command module from the ocean and having the astronauts on the boat seen arriving on shore. The moon footage would need to be filmed in advance so it can be edited. You'd need a way to broadcast it later. You'd have to at least orbit the moon because other countries would be able to see if you sent something into lunar orbit or not. Such a mission would have to be manned. Because you pre-recorded the moon events, you could have the real astronauts on that mission, but mission control would have to know the signals they were receiving aren't from the moon. If you faked the broadcast in a way that could fool mission control, then you have a literal army of technical people working that side.

In a nutshell, there's no way in any variation to pull this off with a small number of people and expect them to stay quiet for more than 50 years.

Let's return for a moment to Bill Kaysing, who worked for Rocketdyne until 1963 and wrote the first book suggesting the mission was faked. His base claim is that the necessary technology didn't exist to send people to the moon and bring them back home. I'll give him a pass on this point because when he left Rocketdyne in 1963, he was correct. The technology of that year wouldn't have allowed it. But he failed to keep up on the advances in technology over the next several years that ultimately made the mission possible. It was hard and it was expensive, but by the time the first people stepped foot on the moon, we very much did have the technology to do it.

Another point: If it was faked, why continue faking it? Achieve the goal and then save money by discontinuing it with the official claim that the mission achieved the goal and was too expensive to continue. If you're going to continue faking it, why not follow up with the next high-profile leap of going to Mars? What better way to hide funding and progress of secret military activities than to shroud them behind the supposed funding of a Mars program?

Overall, a fake moon/Mars program would be the perfect shadow operation to reroute funding to other programs. There'd be little motivation to stop such a program.

Another point that a planner would consider but that conspiracy theorists don't usually think about is a cost-benefit approach and the consideration of failure. What are the consequences if the plan fails? In the case of a faked moon landing, the consequences would be international humiliation and the destruction of credibility from which the country might never recover. Is such a risk worth it compared with the potential benefits?

I'll finish here by returning to the beginning of the chapter: The Soviet Union had the technology and the counterintelligence infrastructure to see whether we really did go to the moon and would've been the first to expose a hoax—not a former technical writer who had self-isolated from information resources, didn't understand the technological advances that were rapidly taking place, lived a transient lifestyle, and wrote a book at his kitchen table.

For these reasons, the moon landing conspiracies fall on the irrational/illogical/unlikely-to-impossible side of our conspiracy spectrum.

CHAPTER 6

AREA 51 & EXTRATERRESTRIAL UFOs

In 2019, someone created a Facebook event calling for the storming of Area 51: "Storm Area 51, They Can't Stop All of Us." Despite the event creator saying it was a joke, the event collected more than 1 million followers, many saying they'd attend. Fortunately, it never materialized.

Why the obsession with Area 51? The base is forever connected to events in Roswell, New Mexico, in 1947, in which a supposed flying saucer crashed and was quickly recovered (and covered up) by the government. The same thing allegedly happened in Aztec, New Mexico, in 1948, when alien technology and alien bodies were supposedly recovered. (It was later exposed as a hoax.) We'll come back to this point at the end of this chapter because believe it or not, a flying saucer might really have crashed in Roswell, New Mexico.

To set this up and tie things together in a way that will make sense (sort of), we must start in June 1947. Rancher W.W. Brazel found some odd debris spread over almost a square mile of his remote ranch near Corona, New Mexico. He gathered mostly tinfoil, rubber, and small wooden beams, with plans to dispose of it later. Little more than two weeks later, the very first "flying saucer" was reported around Mt. Rainier in the state of Washington by private pilot Kenneth Arnold. This story quickly spread throughout the media, causing what has since been called the "flying saucer frenzy" of copycat reports across the United States.

On July 5, 1947, 10 days after the media reports of the flying saucer, Brazel went into town for the first time since discovering the debris and heard the stories about the flying saucer. He decided to gather the debris and took it to the sheriff's office in Roswell. Within days, the finding was reported to the military and representatives showed up to take the debris. A public information officer referred to parts of the debris as a "flying disc," which was later assumed to mean "flying saucer."

What was this debris? Tinfoil, rubber, and pieces of wooden beams seem like odd debris for an advanced alien flying saucer. It was officially listed as a weather balloon, but that wasn't entirely correct either. It's true there was a secret operation the military tried to cover up, but it wasn't what the UFO (unidentified flying object) conspiracy theorists think. It was part of a secret operation called Project Mogul, a program that used weather balloons to launch sound-monitoring equipment high into the atmosphere to listen for evidence of Soviet nuclear tests. This was a short-lived operation from 1947 to 1949, quickly replaced by seismic and atmospheric monitoring systems that did the job better. Project Mogul used sound-monitoring hardware as well as disc-shaped arrays to transmit data back to the ground. They were intended to remain at high altitudes for long periods of time, but there were problems in early development with maintaining stable altitude, and if the altitude increased too much, the expanding balloons would burst, sending the relatively heavy equipment crashing to the ground. This is what was found by Brazel.

There was a story about the finding in the *Roswell Daily Record* on July 9, 1947, but not much of anything was said about the incident for the next 30 years.

Several months later, in March 1948, two men known to be local con artists claimed to have seen a UFO crash about 12 miles outside of Aztec, New Mexico. They claimed the military quickly came and took the remains, which included up to 16 alien bodies. The two men used this as the basis for selling "secret alien technology" that could locate gas, oil, and gold. These pieces of advanced alien technology turned out to be made of aluminum. In 1953, the two men were convicted of fraud.

All this disappeared from the public consciousness until the UFO craze of the 1970s, when various authors claimed the US government possessed secret alien technology and possibly even alien bodies. What better evidence to support these claims than the long-forgotten events from New Mexico? And so was born the legend of Roswell (even though none of the events occurred in Roswell).

What spurred this interest? An increase in UFO sightings in the southwest United States and supposed secret operations going on at the air force facility at Groom Lake in Lincoln County, Nevada, northwest of Las Vegas. It was a very isolated location, appropriate for working on secret projects but also for creating public suspicion.

There's no agreement on where the name Area 51 comes from. A CIA document from the Vietnam era refers to an Area 51, but it doesn't specify the location. The base itself has gone by many nicknames, including The Ranch, Paradise Ranch, and Dreamland. The more official names are simply Homey Airport and Groom Lake. It was never a “secret” base, but it wasn’t officially recognized until a series of documents were declassified in 2013 following a Freedom of Information Act (FOIA) request. The government confirmed that many of the operations conducted there are considered secret and classified, which would make sense given its remote location and the relative ease of security because of the lack of any significant civilian population nearby. If someone is getting too close, it’s easy to spot them.

As I’ll note in the last section of this chapter, many of the UFO reports in that region during the 1950s and into the 1970s were likely because of test flights of experimental aircraft originating from that facility. But before we get into that, let’s put several of the Area 51 conspiracies on our conspiracy spectrum.

The easiest first: Area 51 facility exists, it’s a military operation, and top secret activities are carried out there. This stopped being a conspiracy in 2013 with the release of documents confirming the base and its hosting of secret and classified operations. So the rumor is confirmed. It no longer meets our criteria as a conspiracy.

Next: There’s secret alien technology, including the remains of aliens, stored and being studied at Area 51. This one is problematic for many reasons. The biggest is that travel between stars would require science fiction technology—a convenient bucket the theorists can turn to when their theories are questioned. But it’s a bucket that causes its own problems.

For example, say you’re an advanced alien species with technology far beyond anything on Earth—possibly beyond anything Earthlings can imagine—but you have a relatively small flying saucer that crashes in a remote location and you can’t get to it and retrieve any debris or bodies before the lowly Earthlings find it? Why is such advanced technology not good enough to prevent humans from seeing it? In the case of the Mt. Rainier sighting, why are you flying around a mountain in daylight hours at an altitude where you can potentially be seen by thousands of people?

And what's your obsession with the United States? Most UFO sightings in the world are in the United States and they all started after the media reported the first sighting around Mt. Rainier. There were no verified sightings in the modern era prior to that, no sightings of the Mt. Rainier UFO from anyone on the ground, and no reported sightings following that incident until it was reported in the mass media—and then literally hundreds of reported sightings in a short period of time.

There's another problem with the sightings after Mt. Rainier and the role of the media in spreading it: The images the media chose to show with the story were a stereotypical flying saucer: round, silver, with a circular bulge on the top. This isn't quite the same thing Arnold reported in his first sighting. He did use the words "saucer," "disc," and "plate," but his description was a mostly flat object that was rounded in the back and came to a point in the front. Nothing like the images the mass media were reporting. Why is this important? Because the rash of reports that followed matched the pictures in the media more than the report by Arnold.

We need to step over to the curb for a moment and talk about the power of suggestion and the ability of the media to plant mass suggestion. If you were outside looking at clouds, simply admiring their shapes, you might not see things in the clouds, but if I then pointed at one and said "That one looks like a rabbit," you'd now see its similarity to a rabbit when you hadn't seen the similarity before. This also happened with the rash of "satanic backward messages" people were hearing on rock albums in the 1970s, which fizzled out when others noted similar satanic messages in Christian music.

If I play a record backward, you're likely to hear backward noise, but if I tell you to listen for specific words, you're likely to hear those words.

The field of psychology experienced a similar effect related to what was once known as multiple personality disorder (MPD) after the publication of the book *Sybil* in 1973 and the movie in 1976. MPD was extremely rare prior to 1973. There had been fewer than 100 documented cases in history and the specific case of Sybil (which later turned out to be fabricated) was the first of its kind. After the book and movie were released, there was an explosion of cases, mostly in the United States, and almost all the cases were like Sybil.

With this in mind, we go back to flying saucers and address the elephant in the room: These people were seeing *something*. What was it? There are many natural and man-made phenomena that from the ground can look like a flying saucer, such as hot-air balloons, weather balloons, and lenticular clouds. In 2021, SpaceX caused a flurry of UFO reports every time they launched a new batch of satellites for their Starlink satellite program. It reached a point where some conspiracy theorists claimed there was no Starlink and that the launches were fake, intended to cover up alien activity and the mass movement of alien spacecraft. This was simply and easily debunked by the number of SpaceX enthusiasts who'd personally witnessed the Starlink launches.

Fata Morgana, more generally referred to as "atmospheric ducting," is an atmospheric effect that produces mirages in the air of objects or light effects on the ground. Some suggest this to be the cause of many UFO reports.

Other sightings are often uncovered as hoaxes meant to draw attention. All these factors combined explain roughly three-quarters of all UFO reports. Obviously, that leaves a quarter that aren't explained. What could they be? One clue is in the fluctuating reports of the shapes of UFOs between the 1940s and 1970s—from round saucer-like objects to triangle-shaped or cigar-shaped objects. This fluctuation correlates almost perfectly with the designs of top secret aircraft being test-flown during those decades—many of them at Area 51. We'll get to some of those projects shortly.

Another problem with the idea of aliens visiting us from other planets is one of timing. Given the size and age of the universe, it's very likely other intelligent species could evolve but not necessarily in the timeline we've evolved. In our entire history, we've had the technology to listen to space and explore space for a very short time, and any message we might receive will be millions of years old by the time we hear it. Are those people still around? Similarly, if other species have located us by our transmissions, they'd have to be very close because our first radio and TV signals haven't reached very far into space yet. If there are other intelligent species in the universe at this very moment, it's unlikely they know we exist—just as we don't know they exist.

But why not play with this idea for a moment? Take our project management approach and apply it to aliens visiting Earth. What's the goal and are their methods rational?

They have the technology to make it here from somewhere quite distant. There must be something about us that attracted them. Because they haven't publicly announced themselves or decided to either conquer us or openly share their technology, we'd have to assume the goal is either observation or secret infiltration of our culture.

They seem to be doing fairly well with discreet observation, except for ships sometimes seen flying around at night—visible because of bright lights or flashing lights—and ships sometimes being seen briefly near populated areas. But you'd think there'd be better technology and planning to avoid such oversight. Even we lowly humans with our comparatively primitive technology have materials that are highly light absorbing and could easily make a spaceship nearly invisible at night.

In a nutshell, when you think about the kind of advanced civilization that would have the technology to come here, would they be so obvious yet at the same time seem to want to stay secret? Would our government be the only one who knows about them?

As you can tell, there are too many variables and it's easy to justify any alien conspiracy by jumping into convenient science fiction buckets of theoretical and unproven science. But the government has admitted many times over the years—and in recent years released some previously confidential reports—about the existence of UFOs. Is that proof aliens are among us?

Not at all. First and foremost, when the government says UFO, they literally mean "unidentified flying object"—an object in the sky or in orbit of which they don't know the source. This could be anything. In fact, if the government knew any of these sightings were from another planet, then technically they wouldn't be unidentified anymore.

The media, especially the media associated with conspiracy theories, tend to focus on the number of reports by the general public with little follow-up as to the explanation. For example, the UFO reports generated by Starlink satellite launches are never officially registered because officials know right away what they are.

I know we've been all over the board so far. Let's start taking specific conspiracy theories and placing them on our spectrum. We'll start with the most basic: The US government has evidence that extraterrestrials exist—either possessing hardware, technology, or even bodies—and is keeping that information from the general public.

There are multiple goals we could consider. First, we're acquiring advanced technology from them and want to keep it from our enemies. Second, they want to protect society from the knowledge we're not alone. Why would this be a motivation? Because much of our culture finds comfort in the idea we're alone in the universe and the idea of other intelligent species would challenge many world religions as well as spark fear. Think about how many movies have presented extraterrestrials as hostile species with the intention of enslaving or destroying us. An episode of *Star Trek: The Next Generation* addressed this issue. The *Enterprise* crew was observing a planet that was on the verge of developing warp drive. During observation, they were accidentally discovered. At the end of the episode, the leader of the extraterrestrial world, who had learned about the *Enterprise* and the Federation, asked them to leave, deciding his people weren't yet ready to realize they weren't the center of the universe. It's not hard to imagine people on Earth would have a similar problem.

This conspiracy does have a rational goal. Its process of keeping the information secret is a good approach to the goal. The problem with this one is that there's no evidence of sudden leaps in technology that the United States kept to itself. Computer tech has spread worldwide and it isn't an unusual or unexpected progression of the technology that preceded it. Tubes, then transistors, then microcircuits are a rational technological progression that all stem from the basic advances in electricity and the development of the lightbulb.

Although the conspiracy itself would seem to fall on the rational end of the spectrum, the problems with conveniently encountering an intelligent alien species at just the right time and the United States being the only one to discover them cause this conspiracy to slide to the unlikely end of our spectrum.

Here's a conspiracy that's addressed less often but is much more valid: The US military itself created and propagated the idea of alien UFOs and alien technology as a cover to protect their own secret projects. Secret aircraft at some point must be test-flown, so once they're in the air, there's always the chance someone will see it. So how to explain it? Blow it off as UFO reports and dismiss witnesses and UFO conspiracy theorists as irrational in order to prevent hostile nations from believing that such reports might be of genuine experimental aircraft.

This one is on the rational end of our spectrum. It has the obvious goal of protecting the confidentiality of secret projects. The method of promoting public misinformation is a very good approach to achieving the goal, and because we're talking about already secure and secret operations, it wouldn't take many people to carry it out. This is not only a valid "conspiracy," but it's also very likely. Why is it less popular among UFO conspiracy theorists? You can probably guess. It dismisses the idea that extraterrestrials exist and are among us. This idea alone is very popular in conspiracy circles and many resist letting go of it.

Let's tie together many different elements we've covered by talking about some of the secret operations that were really being carried out at Area 51 between the 1950s and 1980s. How do we know these operations were really happening? Because they've since been declassified. Keep in mind an earlier point: The reported shapes of UFOs changed over the decades and those changes correlate very strongly with the shapes of experimental aircraft being developed secretly.

If you're familiar with military aviation, especially experimental aircraft, when I mention triangular-shaped UFOs, you might be thinking of a flying wing. Many people today are familiar with the B-2 Spirit, or Stealth Bomber, but there were attempts at building tailless fixed-wing aircraft well before World War II. As several of these designs were test-flown in the 1950s, they were spotted by civilians and reported as UFOs. This is to be expected considering how drastically the designs varied from the typical aircraft of the time. Keep in mind what the general public pictured from the 1940s through the 1960s when they thought of airplanes: very typical cylindrical bodies with tails and large wings. Many of the planes we're about to cover deviated so much from that expectation that they could be taken for nothing other than UFOs, and when they were spotted and reported, the military would understandably not confirm they were experimental aircraft and instead list them as unsolved or unknown.

The air force had a program called Project Blue Book that investigated UFO sightings and would compare sightings with test flights of known and secret experimental aircraft. Probably most UFO reports, especially in the southwestern United States, resulted from Project Oxcart, established in 1959 for the purpose of producing faster planes that could fly at extreme altitudes and planes that could avoid radar detection. These designs were mostly intended for spy planes, but even the later Stealth Bomber programs had their roots in this program.

The U-2 spy plane began development in Project Aquatone in 1955 but was later absorbed into Project Oxcart. This was one of the first secret projects to be done at Area 51 because the location gave the program greater potential for secrecy. The U-2 caused multiple UFO reports because it flew at such extremely high altitudes. When it passed over during the hours after sunset, it would be at a high enough altitude to still be in sunlight. Its long wings would reflect the sunlight and make it look like a fast-moving ball of fire.

The A-12, tested at Area 51, was long, thin, and black, and it moved faster than any other aircraft at the time. If you were driving through the desert and happened to see it fly over, it looked like a fast cigar-shaped object zipping across the sky. The plane that followed it, the SR-71 Blackbird, produced even more cigar-shaped UFO reports, even from some military pilots who were unaware it existed. It had a similar shape but much greater speed—it was being flown as early as 1962 but still holds the record for the fastest air-breathing aircraft—so if it buzzed over you on a test flight, you wouldn't see it for long and it looked like nothing you had ever seen before in real life or movies. It could be nothing but a UFO.

The big kicker was Project 1794—one of several projects by the United States and in cooperation with the Canadian military to develop an actual flying saucer. Pieces of this program have been declassified over the years, with the biggest information dump in 2008. Some of the designs never made it past the design phase, but it seems some were built and tested.

Does this sound like something that should be on the irrational and unlikely end of our spectrum? No. The public idea of a flying saucer—a spaceship capable of near-light or faster-than-light travel—is definitely on the irrational end of the scale because it requires science fiction leaps in technology that at the moment only exist theoretically, but a flying saucer as a simple aircraft isn't science fiction—it's completely feasible. Potentially, a saucer design could result in a craft capable of extreme supersonic speeds (between Mach 3 and Mach 4) and would also have the advantage of being able to launch vertically and hover. Turns out, it also has the unfortunate weakness of being very unstable and virtually impossible to recover once stability is lost.

What better source of UFO sightings than an actual flying saucer hovering around an isolated location in the country and then zipping away at an impressive speed? Indeed, it seems this was happening a lot in the 1960s. If you lived in a low-density area with an air force base nearby, you might have seen a higher-than-normal number of UFO reports around your area from that decade.

By no surprise, when top secret experimental aircraft are being test-flown, they'll sometimes crash. What would be the expected military response to a highly secret project crashing? Not surprising at all that they'd close off the area, collect as much wreckage as possible, and not disclose the true nature of what they were doing there. Not hard to see why conspiracies would fly afterward.

To sum up, where do we fall on these conspiracy theories? Let's recap.

The idea that Area 51 exists and is a facility where secret programs are developed and carried out? Not even a conspiracy. Declassified documents have proven this is true.

There are craft of alien origin and alien bodies stored at Area 51? This one falls on the unlikely side of our spectrum, most problematically because of the lack of any evidence that there are known intelligent species in the universe. If there are, why are they interested in us and why are they focusing on the United States (where the majority of global UFO reports are made)?

The other conspiracy theories centering around Area 51 are too numerous to cover individually, but all of them fall on the unlikely and sometimes irrational side of our spectrum. Secret machines that can control the weather. Time- or dimensional-travel machines. Mind-control machines. All these require science fiction leaps of technology that we currently don't have and, in some cases, are thought to be impossible.

With those issues covered, we can put this one to bed and head to the event that has likely produced more conspiracy theories than any other single event: the terrorist attacks on the United States on September 11, 2001.

CHAPTER 7

SEPTEMBER 11, 2001

Of all the events we're looking at, none have spawned as many conspiracy theories as the 9/11 attacks in the United States, mostly around the collapse of the World Trade Center (WTC) in New York City. This gives us our best opportunity to look at the spectrum of conspiracies—from possible to impossible and from rational to science fiction—related to a single event.

What all these conspiracies share is the belief that the attacks were an inside job. This ranges from believing the US government knew it was going to happen and allowed it to the extreme view that it was government agents—not foreign terrorists—who carried out the attacks. As mentioned in Chapter 2, the historical support for this belief is Operation Northwoods in 1962, which proposed staging terrorist attacks in the United States and connecting the attacks to Cuba to nationally and internationally validate an open military assault on Cuba.

Let's start first with the official account of what happened that day. September 11, 2001: Two flights leave from Logan International Airport in Boston, Massachusetts, both bound for Los Angeles, California. American Airlines Flight 11 took off at 7:59 a.m. and United Airlines Flight 175 took off at 8:14 a.m. American Airlines Flight 77 departed Washington Dulles International Airport six minutes later at 8:20 a.m., also bound for Los Angeles. United Airlines Flight 93 departed Newark International Airport in New Jersey at 8:42 a.m., bound for San Francisco, California. All four planes were hijacked by terrorists minutes after takeoff.

At 8:46 a.m., Flight 11 struck the North Tower of the WTC. Seventeen minutes later, at 9:03 a.m., with multiple live cameras pointed at the WTC, Flight 175 struck the South Tower. At 9:37 a.m., Flight 77 struck the west wall of the Pentagon in Arlington, Virginia. At 10:03 a.m., Flight 93 crashed in a field in Stonycreek Township near Shanksville, Pennsylvania.

The South Tower of the WTC (the second one struck) collapsed at 9:59 a.m., followed by the North Tower at 10:28 a.m., completely destroying several buildings in the WTC complex and seriously damaging others, including 7 WTC (Tower 7), which, after sustaining significant damage to 18 lower floors and hours of uncontrolled fires and escalating internal collapses, fully collapsed at 5:21 p.m.

It was quickly determined that the terrorist group Al-Qaeda was responsible for the attacks. Flight 93 was apparently brought down by the terrorists when it became obvious the passengers were going to gain control of the plane before it could reach its target (later determined to be the US Capitol in Washington, DC).

Damage to the heat insulation and support structure in the WTC led to the weakening of the structure, which resulted in the collapses of both struck buildings and 7 WTC.

The crews, passengers, and hijackers on the planes all died as well as 2,606 people on the ground in and around the WTC and 125 people in the Pentagon.

That's the official story. But why so many conspiracy theories? Why such a lack of trust in the official reports? And where did the conspiracy theories come from?

The 9/11 attacks were obviously a huge story, covered in real time as events unfolded. With so much coverage and so much shock, fear, and anger, people were hungry for details and explanations. Many later conspiracy theories were rooted in the rumors, false reports, and misinformation that spread during the day. For example, we know now that only four planes were hijacked, but during the day, there were reports of up to eight hijacked planes, including one supposedly hijacked out of Pittsburgh. There were false reports of a hijacked plane simply circling the DC metro area. When the first survivors of the tower collapse were found, there were reports they'd ridden the roof to the ground as the towers collapsed. There were rumors of car bombs being set off outside the State Department headquarters and various other locations around Washington, DC. All these accounts came from rumors being spread by people without firsthand knowledge of actual events.

This early misreporting is where conspiracies are born. People take these early reports and claim they're accurate, and later information is an attempt to cover up the real information. This will play a big role in Chapter 8, when I cover school shooting conspiracies and "the truthers."

As in every chapter, we'll put conspiracy theories on a spectrum from rational/probable to irrational/improbable. Let's start the 9/11 conspiracies at the rational/probable end and work our way toward the dark side

Notice that you rarely hear about the rational theories because, to be honest, rational is boring. Because it's rational, there's a greater expectation for confirming evidence, whereas the irrational is exciting and requires no real evidence; it creates its own evidence.

At the far end of the "rational" side of the spectrum is the simple belief that the Bush administration knew the attacks were going to happen, could have prevented them, and allowed them to happen. What would be the goal? To open the door for military intervention in the Middle East to take out the Taliban in Afghanistan and Saddam Hussein in Iraq. Then the United States could replace them with more "cooperative" leadership. Almost all 9/11 conspiracies share this common goal: US-endorsed or excused military action in the Middle East.

Does this theory achieve the goal? Yes. Would it involve very many people? Mostly people within national security and intelligence circles who are already good at keeping secrets. There's no logical problem to this theory—only a moral one: The government allowing the deaths of thousands of citizens, which is supported under the umbrella of "collateral damage."

What if we move a little further along the spectrum? Still on the rational side but with more parties involved.

Another theory is that the US government conspired with a foreign agent, either Al-Qaeda itself or the Saudi Arabian government, which then turned to Al-Qaeda to carry out the attacks for the same purpose mentioned earlier. In this scenario, Osama bin Laden wanted the United States to take out the specific sect of the Taliban that was ruling Afghanistan, but the United States couldn't take down a foreign government with open military action simply because they didn't like them. They needed a direct threat to rationalize the action—very similar to the problem the Kennedy administration faced when it wanted to take out Fidel Castro.

You might be wondering how these can be considered rational theories given the loss of innocent lives. We can call them rational because they don't require any strange physics and don't involve as many people as the theories we'll talk about next. The argument is that the actual number of civilian deaths was much higher than expected because, within these theories, no one expected the buildings to collapse. The goal was the image of the WTC, the Pentagon, and the Capitol building on fire. As we'll discuss shortly, if the goal is a blank check for military intervention in the Middle East, the collapse of the towers wasn't necessary. The goal was solidly achieved the moment the second plane hit on live TV.

The low collateral damage argument goes this way: The planes that were chosen were flights with typically low occupancy. The first building to be hit would be the one with the lowest occupancy and would be hit higher than the second building to limit the number of people trapped by the fires. The hit on the second building would be delayed, making sure the media were covering the event and people would have time to evacuate the upper floors of the building. The Pentagon was targeted based on the part of the building being renovated and therefore with lower occupancy. If the third target was supposed to be the Capitol, it would've been evacuated long before the plane struck.

So how do these fit into our criteria for a viable conspiracy? They achieve the goal and don't require very many people. In fact, they could involve very few—just a couple high-level government people negotiating. The people who carried out the event didn't even need to know they were part of a conspiracy. Osama bin Laden was the only person in his group who needed to know he was carrying out a plan with the cooperation of the target country. It doesn't require any stretch of logic or science.

Also on the viable and rational side of the spectrum is the theory that Flight 93, which crashed in Pennsylvania, wasn't brought down by the terrorists who feared they were about to lose control of the plane but by the military attempting to prevent the plane from reaching its target.

Would this achieve the goal of preventing the plane from striking a populated area and producing potentially high fatalities on the ground? Yes. The passengers would die anyway when the plane hit its target, so taking it down in a sparsely populated area would reduce fatalities on the ground. Would it involve very many people to keep it covered up? No. Some variations of this conspiracy claim (although with no substantiated proof) that the military has a set of "secret" codes when engaging with civilians to hide the fact they're killing civilians. In one supposedly "leaked" audio between an air force pilot and traffic control, they confirm visual identification of Flight 93 and are told to "avoid the aircraft and move north." Some conspiracy theorists claim this is code to shoot down the aircraft and go radio silent until they're back on the ground.

Are there valid reasons and motivations to cover this up rather than report the truth? Given what the country went through that day, yes. It would be completely reasonable to limit the horror of the day by not reporting that the military intentionally killed 33 passengers and 7 crew on that plane simply to keep it from hitting a government building. In fact, before the official report that the hijackers intentionally crashed the plane to prevent the passengers from gaining control, there were stories that heroic passengers took control of the plane and intentionally crashed it themselves to prevent the hijackers from achieving their goals and hurting innocent people on the ground—a much more noble way to go than being intentionally killed by your own military.

With those in mind, let's venture into some of the theories that are less realistic, less viable, and more likely to occur in the fictional world of a movie or a book. Instead of looking at one complete conspiracy (because there are too many), let's look at popular individual components of these theories and why they're unlikely and unrealistic.

You can probably guess the first one we're going to address: The Twin Towers and 7 WTC were controlled demolitions because those buildings wouldn't otherwise collapse that way.

Why do so many people think buildings wouldn't collapse that way? How would they expect buildings to collapse if they were truly from structural failure?

We return to "cultivation theory." Most of our stored memory of building collapses comes from movies and TV—fictionalized collapses that mostly defy physics in order to maximize dramatic effect. An action hero needs a chance to escape as a structure collapses around them. In the real world, they'd never make it out. Frequently in movies, large structures will "tip over" as they fall in a way that ignores structural integrity and gravity.

Many people claim the WTC fell straight down on its footprint because of how the buildings looked when they first started to collapse: They seemed to go straight down. But if you look at the initial point of collapse, there are smoke and debris falling away from the outside of the building right away as that top mass obliterates everything beneath it. Very quickly, the view of the top of the building vanishes into the cloud being generated by the collapse.

In a controlled demolition, the mass of the building would move down together and you wouldn't have material being blown out the sides. This means the outward appearance of the collapse is exactly what you'd expect from a structural failure. It looks nothing like what you'd expect from a controlled demolition.

A much bigger problem is the belief that controlled demolitions fall straight down. Once structural support fails, gravity takes over and tries to pull any building straight down unless it encounters resistance. In fact, there's no single style of controlled demolition that's consistent in all of them. What makes a collapse "look" like a controlled demolition isn't the way it falls or the speed at which it falls but where it lands on the ground. Different demolitions will be designed to fall in different ways depending on how engineers need the building to fall in order to stay within the desired footprint.

But let's step back and think about how a controlled demolition would've been planned and carried out if that's what happened. A controlled demolition requires a lot of planning. You can't simply place bombs next to supports and expect it to work. A stick of dynamite releases a lot of force, but it releases it in every direction. The inability of a large explosive force to damage a major vertical support structure was demonstrated by the 1993 bombing of the WTC when a large truck bomb was set off in the lower levels of the North Tower in an attempt to bring the tower crashing down. As large as the explosion was, it didn't damage the support infrastructure. This demonstrated that trying to bring one of the towers down by controlled demolition would require explosives designed for the task—and a lot of them. Explosives used in controlled demolitions are designed to send as much force as possible into the structure.

Planning a controlled demolition of the WTC would require access to the blueprints as well as visual inspection of and access to the primary supports. Unlike other skyscrapers of the time, which had most of their support in a series of columns within the building, the WTC towers had some support of the floors supplied by a tube design along the exterior walls, which was why the design of the towers was called "a tube within a tube." This would make detonation plans more complicated. You'd need to find experts who could plan this but also be trusted to go along with the plan of blowing up these buildings, killing innocent people, creating a national trauma—and then never talk about it.

Because the center tube structure was the primary support of vertical weight, that's where you'd most likely put your explosives.

Let's pause for a moment and answer one question: If the goal was to bring down the towers, why take the risk and the effort of planting what would have to be hundreds of charges throughout upper floors of the skyscrapers when if you have access to the materials, all you needed was to blow all the vertical supports on a single lower floor?

The most common answer is: They wanted it to look like the planes caused the collapse. Starting the collapse from the bottom would look suspicious.

This raises a secondary question: If you want it to look like the planes caused the collapse, why would you risk planting explosives on multiple floors and making it look like a controlled demolition when all you need to do is blow the vertical supports on a single floor?

The answer? They had to plant explosives on multiple floors because they wanted the collapse to start at the point the planes hit the buildings and they couldn't be sure of the exact point of impact.

This all creates the deal-breaker question: What sort of explosive could then be used that could be detonated remotely in a controlled pattern yet not be set off accidentally by the impact of the planes or the resulting fires? That's one with no good physics-based answer.

But let's get back to the labor. There were 47 vertical support columns in the interior of the towers. You need direct access to these or enough explosive force to blast through anything in the way, such as walls or the insulating materials around each of the supports. You need to make sure you have access to all these areas and that your explosives will be placed where they won't create suspicion—and you need a functional detonation system coordinating the explosives. The fewer people you involve, the longer it will take and the better chance of keeping it secret. The more people you involve, the shorter the time but the greater risk of someone discussing and exposing your plans.

Finally, given the number of people you're involving in planting explosives in an active public space, you must have a contingency plan in the event it's discovered. Are all plans off if someone finds these explosives and alerts either the authorities or the media? Do you have people in those places of authority to block that information? And how do you get the police or media to go along with a plan that's going to kill police, firefighters, EMTs, and thousands of others but not say anything about it?

See the problem?

Let's go back to our most basic question: What's the goal of the conspiracy? For all these, the goal has been a terrorist attack on US soil to give the United States a blank check for military intervention in the Middle East, but there are other goals associated with the conspiracies around the bombing of the World Trade Center. Some theories suggest there were secret documents or information stored in the towers and 7 WTC and the collapses were an attempt to destroy that information.

But let's ask an obvious question: If you have the number of people you need, operating with the secrecy they need to plant explosives in those buildings, then why not just send them after the specific items you want destroyed? Why keep such sensitive information at those locations in the first place? The fact that you could sneak so many people into those places undetected to plant explosives is reason enough to not keep anything sensitive in those buildings. You should keep such information in more isolated locations where you have greater control over who has access and greater ability to monitor who comes and goes.

If the goal is open military intervention in the Middle East, then destroying the buildings isn't necessary. The televised image of the Pentagon and the Twin Towers on fire, especially the second plane hitting the buildings on live TV, achieved that goal.

There's a similar problem with the collapse of 7 WTC later in the evening. The popular conspiracy theory is that the building was brought down intentionally, again because of secret documents or information stored within the building.

Here's the biggest problem with those theories: If you have enough resources and people to plant explosives, then you have enough to do a hard-target search for whatever it is you want destroyed.

Would the destruction of the building achieve the goal? Maybe—depending on what it is you're trying to destroy. Computer hard drives would likely be destroyed by a building collapse, but there's a chance they'd survive and be discovered in the rubble. The same with documents. Many would be destroyed, but some might survive and be found in the rubble. Destroying the building would be the least predictable and most unreliable way of getting rid of whatever it is in the building you want to destroy. Again, if you have the resources to plant explosives covertly, you'd use those resources to secretly specifically target what you want to destroy.

Some conspiracists say there's no way the building could collapse from "just a few fires." Conspiracy websites ignore photos taken on September 11th of the 18 stories of damage done to the corner of 7 WTC and the fires that went on unchecked. Several times during the day, the mass media reported that people could hear collapses within the building as the fire weakened individual floor supports and floors collapsed. Several times there were erroneous reports that the building was collapsing before the damage reached a point that the primary vertical supports collapsed and the building came down. The erroneous media reports are seen by conspiracy theorists as evidence that the collapse was scripted in advance, but, of course, this would mean the media was in on it and expecting the collapse. There's a problem with that theory: Why would the media need to be in on it at all? They'd simply represent loose ends and extra people who'd have to know about it. If your plan is to bring the building down, why alert the media in advance?

As with the towers, people believe that because the building looked like it came straight down, it must have been a controlled demolition. In fact, the building didn't come straight down; the collapse started in the southeast corner before internally cascading east to west across the building. Again, real-world physics doesn't operate in convenient slow-motion like in the movies. Even if you were in the building at the time, you might have perceived the entire building coming down at once because the progression of the collapsing force would've been so rapid. But if you look at the videos of the collapse of 7 WTC, you can see the irregular angle of collapse by watching the roofline. As the collapse begins, the east side dips a little faster than the rest because this is where the collapse started.

If it was a controlled demolition, when were the explosives placed? There are two variations of the theories: They were set prior to the attacks at the same time explosives were being planted in the Twin Towers or they were set after the attacks in order to bring down the building because of the damage it had sustained and the fear of people finding secret information. There are similar problems of timing with both theories. If they were set prior to the attacks, why not detonate them immediately after the towers collapsed so the collapse would be hidden by the smoke and debris and therefore appear obvious that it was the collapse of the towers that brought the building down? Otherwise, why wait until so much later?

If the explosives were planted in the building after the Twin Towers collapsed, why take the risk of sneaking people into the building during the day when so many cameras were focused on the WTC location? You could wait until after dark, when it would be easier to sneak people in. You'd also wait until after dark to detonate so it would be harder to see if the collapse looked suspicious.

There's a perceptual issue with all these claims of the buildings coming straight down like a controlled demolition: People watched these collapses from cameras very far away from the buildings, which gives a distorted, minimized view of the size of the buildings. When the towers collapsed, it looked like debris stayed close to the building, when in reality, it fell hundreds of feet away from the towers, easily damaging and destroying nearby buildings.

There was no mystery as to why the towers or 7 WTC collapsed. Without fire suppression efforts, it was inevitable.

"But jet fuel can't melt steel!" This is the most common cut-and-paste chant of 9/11 conspiracy theorists. Heat expands and weakens steel; all it needed to do was weaken it enough that it couldn't maintain the weight above it. Heat expansion of the floor supports within 7 WTC was the primary culprit in the floors collapsing and heat plus internal stress took out the vertical supports. In the Twin Towers, sections of the heat insulation around the vertical support columns were ripped away by the impact from the planes, exposing parts of the beams to greater heat, therefore creating greater expansion. When the uninsulated expanding beams met the still-insulated beams that weren't expanding, physics says cracks will start to occur in the beams, and by no surprise, cracked beams can't hold up the same weight as intact beams.

The Pentagon

The most common conspiracy centering on Flight 77, which struck the Pentagon, is that it was a missile, not a plane, that struck the Pentagon.

This theory does fit the qualification of achieving the goal, but it fails catastrophically in our other criteria: How many people would it take to carry out? How many records must be faked to cover it up? Is the conspiracy as it's proposed the best way to carry out the objective? Are there better ways this could be done with a greater chance of success?

Again, consider cultivation theory: Fictional media stored in your memory is sometimes referenced when your brain is looking for answers to real-world events.

Many people expect the hole on the outside of the Pentagon to look like a cardboard cutout of an airplane, like a cartoon character running through a wall. Only the central mass of the plane would have enough force to penetrate the building and that force would diminish as the mass penetrated deeper layers. The wings of the plane, which also contained fuel tanks, would've been instantly destroyed on impact with the ground or the outside of the building, producing the pattern of fires clearly shown in pictures of the event.

This is why the damage and fires on the outside wall of the Pentagon look exactly like you'd expect after an impact by a passenger jet, especially the location of the penetration and the pattern of the fires around it, but look nothing like what a missile would produce.

Where did the missile theory come from in the first place? Again, rumors and erroneous reporting on the day of the attacks. Several people interviewed on September 11th said it *sounded* like a missile or they thought they *heard* a missile. There's no verified evidence of anyone seeing a missile, but there are plenty of accounts of people seeing the aircraft. Nevertheless, some early news reports looking for any new information reported that it might have been a missile that hit the Pentagon. Again, early misinformation was grabbed by conspiracy theorists as truth and all later information and facts, including security images of the plane hitting the building and verified reports by people who saw the plane, were considered cover-ups.

In this conspiracy, the missile versus plane argument is completely meaningless to the goal and would be unnecessarily complex.

The Pentagon isn't in the middle of nowhere; it's in a dense metropolitan area and the attack was in the morning, when, at the very least, hundreds of people could have potentially seen the attack. No one planning such an attack would argue you could hit the Pentagon with a missile but then tell the public it was a plane.

What would it take to fake a plane? We'll address this in more detail in Chapter 8, but this is our introduction to the problem with "crisis actors." You need to bribe people into saying they saw a plane. You need to quiet anyone who saw a missile (potentially hundreds of people). You need to make sure there are no security cameras or individuals with cameras who might pick up the missile. You need to fake the flight, including airline, airport, and air traffic control records, and make sure everyone in those places will go along with your story. You need to fake the passenger roster. This means paying crisis actors to claim to have been the friends and relatives of the people on the planes. You bribe other people into claiming they're extended family and old school buddies. You fake entire biographies, including work history, school history, school records, school photos, family photos, birth certificates, medical records, etc.

See the problem? It would involve too many people and require faking too many records. The people who agreed to play along would have to play this role for the rest of their lives without a single person ever coming forward to expose the truth. If you were really going to fire a missile at the Pentagon, this would be the plan more likely to succeed: Admit it was a missile. Release reports that fragments of the missile were found and seemed to be of foreign construction. The only physical evidence you need to fake is a launch site. It would be easy to fake a mobile launch site in an isolated location several miles away and claim evidence left behind ties it to a terrorist group. That involves very few people and is arguably better at achieving the goal. After the general public had witnessed a plane strike the WTC on live TV, it would escalate the terror even more to make people believe terrorists had missiles at their disposal within the country and could strike buildings.

This leads to our last conspiracy theory category related to the 9/11 attacks and transitions to Chapter 8: the truthers. The truthers are mostly associated with believing mass shootings are false flag events staged by crisis actors, but their roots are in the 9/11 conspiracies.

Their primary belief is that no one (or at most very few people) died in the attacks. How could that be? They believe there were no people on the planes and that the planes were all automated and flown remotely. The Twin Towers had been evacuated prior to the attack by mysterious fire alarms and everyone in the Pentagon had been evacuated from the sections that had been hit. If the planes were empty, why take down Flight 93? Because it stopped responding to remote operation and then either crashed on its own or was shot down by the military once control was lost.

We don't have to spend much time on this because it has the same problem as faking the flight that hit the Pentagon, but instead of only faking the entire life histories of 59 people and their families and friends, you'd be faking almost 3,000 people.

Why would people need to believe no one died? Obviously, the thought of nearly 3,000 people perishing in the manner they did on what was supposed to be just a typical workday is nightmarish. It hurts to think about it. One way to avoid feeling that pain and fear is to believe it didn't really happen to anyone. We'll address this point further in Chapter 8.

One variation of the empty planes theory is that the flights and passenger rosters were genuine, but all the people were removed from the planes before takeoff, then taken to secret locations, where they were later killed.

Is that the best way to achieve the goal of getting rid of the passengers? Obviously not. The best way would be to leave them on the planes because they'd be crashed into buildings anyway. If you're worried about passengers trying to take control of the planes, then release an odorless gas into the planes as soon as you're in the air to incapacitate everyone until the planes are destroyed.

How would this belief ease the terror of thinking about the deaths of the people on the planes? It changes the manner of death from something obviously horrific to something secret that can easily be ignored or assumed to be more humane.

We now have the foundation for possibly the most bizarre category of conspiracy belief: false flag mass shootings and the truthers. Let's head down that rabbit hole.

CHAPTER 8

MASS SHOOTINGS, FALSE FLAGS & THE TRUTHERS

A "false flag" event is anything real or staged in which the purpose is either propaganda or to place blame for the event on a specific person or group. By definition, the group carrying out or staging the event protects their identities and remains secret. Mentioned earlier, Operation Northwoods in the 1960s—the proposal to stage supposed terrorist attacks in the United States and blame it on Cuba—would've been a false flag operation because the United States would've been secretly attacking itself while placing the blame elsewhere.

There are a series of conspiracy theories wrapped around false flags and some of the specific false flag claims we'll cover, but we'll start with two of the psychological components that might cause a conspiracy theorist to believe in false flag events. The first component is denial and I must give a cautious nod to Sigmund Freud because it's his term. Freud was a great observer of human behavior, but his theories failed to explain why we engage in certain or specific behaviors. So although we no longer consider buried unconscious anxieties as the motivations for these behaviors, we still use much of his terminology.

You're probably familiar with the image of three monkeys with hands over their eyes, ears, and mouths, representing the principle "See no evil, hear no evil, speak no evil." They can also be applied to denial: "I don't want to see it, I don't want to hear about it, I don't want to talk about it." You can also picture the familiar ostrich with its head in the sand, tuning out the reality around it. Denial isn't about shutting out information in general; it's about shutting out information that challenges our beliefs or that creates emotional distress. When something terrible has happened in the world and it hurts to think about it, the easiest way to avoid the pain is to believe it didn't really happen.

A second component is survival related: Our need to feel safe or in general have a sense of security. It makes sense, then, that the thought of random people deciding to shoot up the grocery store while I'm shopping or my child's school while they're there or hijack my flight and crash it is terrifying. They set off a sense of threat. However, if I believe those events are staged or faked, it means there's no threat to me or my loved ones in our day-to-day lives. It's a very comforting way to view the world and one more likely to be found among people who rate high in fear-sensitivity or are motivated by strong feelings of insecurity.

This brings us to the truthers: people who believe many mass shootings and mass killings are staged events in which no one really died or, at the very least, far fewer people died than what's reported by the media. This began with the 9/11 attacks in New York City, in which there were later claims that the buildings had been evacuated by mysterious fire alarms either before the planes struck or before the buildings collapsed. These beliefs were often paired with the claim that the planes were empty. You can see why this would be an appealing view for people who are uncomfortable with imagining the true horror of dying in such an event.

The big push by the truthers, however, was the shooting at Sandy Hook Elementary School in Newtown, Connecticut. As with the other conspiracies we've covered, we'll start with the official account of what happened before covering the conspiracies.

I won't go into excruciating detail because it's a horrific event to imagine, but we need to address some uncomfortable details that are key to the reason conspiracy theories quickly emerged.

On December 14, 2012, at 9:35 a.m., 20-year-old Adam Lanza entered Sandy Hook Elementary School armed with two rifles and a handgun. After shooting through a glass panel near the locked front entrance, Lanza killed the school principal and a school psychologist before moving on to two first-grade classrooms. In the span of roughly 5 minutes, Lanza killed 20 students (all first-graders) and 6 staff members, including the principal, two teachers, and two teaching assistants. By the time police entered the building, Lanza had killed himself with a single gunshot to the head.

The motive? We can never be completely certain because Lanza killed himself, but his history leaves the door open for speculation. Lanza was diagnosed very early with developmental problems. He was first diagnosed with autism spectrum disorder, later with Asperger's syndrome (which today is included on the autism spectrum), and with depression, anxiety, and obsessive-compulsive disorder. These factors caused his school attendance to be sporadic, but what seemed to tip the scales in a bad direction was the divorce of his parents in 2009 and his mother's struggles to deal with her son's needs alone. She reportedly became a "gun enthusiast," collecting multiple weapons and ammunition, supposedly out of concern for being able to protect herself and her son alone. She also became more physically and emotionally distant in her day-to-day interactions with her son, as he became more withdrawn and spent most of his day in his room on the internet and watching videos. Authorities later revealed the mother and son communicated frequently by text and email despite living in the same house.

The crisis point was the mother's decision to sell their house. Understanding her son's needs and the problems he'd have moving to a new environment, she intended to purchase a recreational vehicle and gradually move him into it to become comfortable in the environment before selling the house. Leading up to this time, Lanza had become obsessed with videos and documentaries about mass shootings in general and school shootings specifically.

It wouldn't be out of the question to suggest that a combination of factors—social and emotional withdrawal, anger at his mother, fear of leaving his familiar isolated environment, and suicidal ideation—combined to tip him toward violence.

But why Sandy Hook? And why first-graders? Lanza had attended Sandy Hook for almost four years during elementary school; it wasn't a good experience for him, and based on some of his writings that were found later, he might have thought he was saving the children from living the kind of life he'd lived. Alternatively, he could have been teased or bullied by kids when he was a child attending the school and chose it as a sort of revenge for that treatment, perceiving elementary school children as cruel. Or maybe the first-grade classrooms just happened to be the first ones he reached. It could also be that the specific school didn't matter; a school shooting was his chosen final act and Sandy Hook was simply the nearest school.

Before we start picking apart the "false flag" conspiracy theories, I need to address one other event in this genre: the 2017 Las Vegas shooting at the Route 91 Harvest country music festival—the deadliest mass shooting by a single individual in US history (at the time of this writing).

On the evening of October 1, 2017, from his suites on the 32nd floor of the Mandalay Bay hotel, 64-year-old Stephen Paddock began firing on the crowd attending the music festival. He fired more than 1,000 shots, killing 60 people and wounding 411. An additional 400 people were wounded during the ensuing panic as people tried to flee. By the time police located and entered his room, he'd killed himself.

He left nothing behind to indicate a motive, and other than having lost a lot of money the previous year in gambling, he showed no other indicators of someone who'd carry out such an action. Later surveillance images, interviews with friends, and tracking his history over the preceding year led investigators to believe he'd scouted several locations for a potential shooting and even brought weapons to several of those locations, but why he waited until the music festival will never be known.

I include this one because it's also a target of truthers who believe it was a false flag event. It's also an example of how erroneous early reports can be adopted by conspiracy theorists as truth, while later more accurate reports are considered a cover-up. In this case, police radio conversations and some body camera video reveal the chaos as the shooting was taking place and chronicle the police believing the shooting was coming from a much lower floor in the hotel rather than the 32nd. How could police make such an error? In a situation like that, when you're seeking cover and also trying to identify the source, you don't get a lot of good looks at the source of the gunfire. In Las Vegas, there are many distracting lights that from a distance, especially when reflecting in windows, might be confused for the barrel flash of gunfire. This seems to have been the case.

There are two general and contradictory conspiracies that formed after the shooting. One is that it was completely staged. There were no actual victims; all the supposed victims and direct witnesses were crisis actors. The other is that there was an actual shooting, but Paddock was set up to take the fall while an actual shooter fired the shots from a lower-floor window. Our project management approach has logical problems with both. We'll first address the latter theory because it's unique to this specific shooting compared with most other mass shootings.

We can immediately eliminate part of this conspiracy: that there was another shooter on a lower floor. If you were going to set up a scenario in which you're framing someone else as the shooter, there's no scenario in which you'd put the actual shooter on a lower floor. The trajectory would be poor and there's no chance that people at ground level wouldn't see and hear it. It would be too easy for security to quickly identify and access the room. A final nail in the coffin of this theory is the lack of any broken windows at the hotel other than those Paddock broke out—unless they were quickly replaced, which creates its own problems of getting the people and resources to that room without being noticed. Why would doing that be part of your plan?

An alternative version of this theory? The shooter was in Paddock's room and Paddock was killed to be left behind as the assumed shooter. On the surface, this seems like it would be on the rational side of the spectrum, except for the problem of the shooter escaping the floor when escape routes had been limited and there were already people entering the floor from the only available access route.

What about the theory that there were no deaths and it was a faked event using crisis actors as victims and witnesses? This point can't be repeated enough: Any conspiracy theory that involves crisis actors is an automatic no. It's an instant ticket to the irrational/impossible end of the conspiracy spectrum. No one with the power or resources to carry out a conspiracy of such scale would use crisis actors; they're loose ends over whom you have limited control and you're expecting them to play that role for the rest of their lives and never reveal it. Remember Operation Northwoods? Many of those plans were rejected because they'd involve too many people outside the circle of security. This would be a primary concern in putting together a secret plan.

To use Sandy Hook as an example, if none of the victims were real people, it would require faking school records, birth records, family histories, and, in the case of the teachers, education records. In addition to the crisis actors, you have to convince literally hundreds of other people to claim to be the friends and family of these people, so you need to fake family pictures and vacation pictures. The more records you fake, the further back you have to go and the more people who need to become involved. Everyone at the school would have to be in on it because they'd know it wasn't a real class.

First responders would also have to be in on it because there'd be no real bodies, and if the claim is that the first responders are crisis actors themselves, then what about the real first responders in the community? Wouldn't the police wonder who these other "police" were at the scene of a supposed mass shooting of children? Wouldn't they say something about it? You also need to convince first-grade children to claim to be some of the survivors who saw their classmates killed and these children would stick to this story for the rest of their lives, so not one of the people approached to be crisis actors would ever come clean and reveal it. When you take a project management approach to the plan and consider all the different components it would involve and the huge cast of characters that would be necessary to carry it out, it's not just unlikely; it's functionally impossible.

An alternate theory that does believe shootings really occur and victims really perish suggests that the shooters have been brainwashed to carry out the acts. A similar theory is often proposed regarding Lee Harvey Oswald and the Kennedy assassination. To address this, we need to sidestep into the concepts of brainwashing and cults because they apply here and will apply even more in Chapter 9 on the QAnon conspiracies.

Is "brainwashing" as the general public thinks of it a real thing? Not really. The public perception of "cult" and "brainwashing" comes out of the United States in the 1950s and 1960s as people were adopting beliefs so far removed from the socialized norms of the time that people couldn't understand how others could come to hold such beliefs. For example, joining a fringe religious group when one had been socialized and raised within mainstream Christianity was thought to require brainwashing. It should be noted that in the 1950s, the US government itself pushed Christianity as a religious norm (such as adding "under God" to the Pledge of Allegiance and "In God We Trust" on money) as a way to morally separate the United States from the supposedly "godless" Soviet Union at the height of tensions between those countries.

The root of brainwashing comes from films released during the Korean War of US prisoners of war renouncing US culture and capitalism and claiming to prefer Communism. These soldiers were making these statements under duress to avoid torture and death. But in the United States, the statements were taken as genuine, so the common explanation was some sort of mental control or manipulation that became popularly known as brainwashing. The government itself had tremendous motivation to promote the idea of brainwashing to emphasize that the socialized norms citizens were encouraged to accept were intuitively the only correct way to think and live. To believe anything else must be a product of either coercion or mental illness.

This idea was further popularized by Hollywood in the 1962 film *The Manchurian Candidate*, in which a decorated war hero was programmed to carry out specific commands when triggered by seeing the queen of diamonds in a deck of cards. Ultimately, that person was manipulated to assassinate a presidential candidate. It's not hard to understand why this movie would fuel many conspiracy theories when President Kennedy was assassinated the following year. Just as the 1996 movie *The Long Kiss Goodnight* about a secret CIA plan to fake a terrorist attack on the United States helped fuel conspiracies about the 9/11 attacks.

If it's not brainwashing, then what causes people to reject the socialized norms of their upbringing in such extreme ways? Two factors are most common: A bad experience with the socialized norms weakens their hold on us and the new belief satisfies a strong emotional need. Once a belief becomes attached to emotional comfort or our sense of security, our brains spend a lot of resources justifying them and protecting them from outside information and criticism. This is why a belief is very hard to change once it's emotionally embraced.

Any strongly held belief, especially religious and political beliefs, can be interpreted as brainwashing or cult behavior because once we identify with a group, we'll hold very strongly to the beliefs of that group and defend them.

In 1956, psychologist Leon Festinger published *When Prophecy Fails: A Social and Psychological Study of a Modern Group That Predicted the Destruction of the World*. Festinger had infiltrated an end-of-the-world cult to study the beliefs and rationalizations within the group—specifically, what would happen within the group when the world didn't end at the predicted time. Did the group become disillusioned and fall apart when the world didn't end? Some members did leave, but overall, the group became even *more* committed to their beliefs. How could this be?

None of us want to be wrong or believe we could be easily fooled, so when a prediction fails, we'll jump on board with any explanation that helps us hang on to the belief while explaining the failure. Therefore, when predictions of specific dates come and go without anything happening, followers will readily jump on board with the next prediction. We'll see more recent examples of this in Chapter 9 when we cover QAnon and its various date-specific predictions, none of which came to pass.

To a degree, you can predict someone's willingness to fall in with a belief if you know what's emotionally important to them and what they fear. This is the eternal three-step model of getting people to follow you: Make them afraid of something, tell them whom to blame for it, and tell them you can solve it or protect them from it. If you can take people down that path and make it sound rational, you'll get rational people listening and following.

That's a long trip around the block to say that people being brainwashed to carry out a secret plan is on the unlikely and irrational end of our spectrum. Even if it was possible, it would be very high risk with very low probability of success and a tremendous downside if it was discovered.

Before we take the false flag general conspiracy idea and place it along the spectrum, we need to address one more thing: Where did the idea come from that groups would fake mass shootings specifically to turn the public against guns and help generate anti-gun legislation? This idea hasn't been around forever. What happened?

The answer lies in propaganda and fearmongering for political gain inspired by the 1994 assault weapons ban, which was in place for 10 years and which escalated when the ban ended in 2004. Prior to the ban, there had been a series of mass shootings over several years that led to political pressure to restrict access to automatic or semi-automatic weapons. You can see how the connection between mass shootings and "restrictive" gun laws was a simple association for those seeking political influence.

The George W. Bush administration allowed the ban to expire in 2004, which caused a surge in the sale of the previously banned weapons—in many cases by people purchasing the weapons as investments with the expectations the ban would eventually be restored and the value of the weapons would increase. Unfortunately for their investments, this hasn't yet happened. The fear of the ban being restored also helped the gun industry create artificial bumps in sales every time a Democrat won the White House or Democrats took control of either the House or Senate.

It was valuable political propaganda during the 2008 election to assume that if Barack Obama was elected, he'd restore the ban. This was mentioned several times during the campaign, but it wasn't until the Sandy Hook shooting in 2012 that any real effort was made to restore the ban—and those efforts failed.

It's not hard to see how someone could convince people that because mass shootings influenced the first ban, staging mass shootings might be a way to restore the ban.

There are also two sociological/psychological factors that changed during the years of the assault weapons ban: Guns went from being perceived simply as objects and a normalized part of US history to a symbol essential for a sense of freedom and protection. In other words, guns went from an emotionless object to something that represented a deep emotional need for safety.

This was done through propaganda pushed by people seeking personal gain—financial and political. The other factor is 9/11. As much as people in the United States chanted after the attacks that they wouldn't live in fear, we did develop greater fear and a greater sense of risk to self than was present before the attacks. This was most pronounced in the 2002 midterm and 2004 presidential elections when both main parties used the fear of terrorism to try to influence voters.

At the beginning of this chapter, I established that the desire to believe mass shootings are staged is a self-protective mechanism. It makes us feel safer to believe such shootings don't occur randomly. You can see how this desire for safety was impacted by the 9/11 attacks and drove the evolving attitude toward guns. Hollywood also played a role in displaying guns as the ultimate in self-protection regardless of what weapons are being wielded by an enemy. Movies have socialized us to believe the good person always has an advantage over the bad person. Even in a tense and fast-moving environment, the bad person will pause at the right moment and for the right amount of time to allow the good person to react—and the good person's reflexes, reaction time, and aim will always be superior to the bad person's. This has unfortunately resulted in something called "action movie syndrome," in which people put themselves at unnecessary risk because they feel they'll have an advantage or their weapon can protect them from any threat.

Do you know why you hear so many stories about homeowners successfully defending themselves with guns but not stories about how often they fail? Because when they're successful, they survive to tell the tale; when they fail, they don't. And if they fail, the thief usually steals their weapon, leaving no sign that the homeowner ever made an attempt.

Gun culture and weapon psychology are two subjects that could fill their own book, so we can't go into detail with those here, but I'll address one point: Guns in the United States are such a cultural norm and a historical aspect of the culture that it's unrealistic to believe the government is going to abolish the Second Amendment and take away guns during our lifetimes. It wouldn't be functionally possible. So the idea that the government will disarm the public falls on the irrational end of our conspiracy spectrum.

There's an alternate conspiracy theory related to turning the public against guns: The gun rights movement itself, including the National Rifle Association (NRA), is being used to turn the general public away from guns and lead to stricter gun laws. How can this be? By making the entire movement seem irrational, unbending, and dangerous. One of the arguments is that after a mass shooting, rather than show sympathy for the victims, gun rights supporters immediately defend the weapons used in the killing. This creates the perception that they're defending the killer.

How does this alternate theory fit with our project management approach and on our conspiracy spectrum? On the rational side of the spectrum, it would achieve the goal and it wouldn't involve very many people. You wouldn't need to physically infiltrate any of these groups. Instead, simply pour propaganda into the groups and let them do the rest without being aware what they're doing.

With the long-winded part over, let's wrap up this chapter by summarizing where false flag events fit into our criteria:

- It would involve too many people.
- There's a low probability of success. It's not an effective way to achieve the goal.
- Many other options would achieve the same goal with fewer people.

- The risk is extremely high.
- There's a massive downside if it were exposed. Indeed, it's realistically impossible to keep it from being discovered.
- The primary motivation of turning public attitudes away from guns and leading to the disarming of the population isn't practical.
- Given that after every mass shooting there are claims the shooting is a staged false flag event, it assumes real mass shootings never occur; therefore, all recorded victims of mass shootings are fake and all survivors and witnesses are paid crisis actors playing their roles for the rest of their lives.

With false flag shootings and the truthers behind us, it's time to dive into the all-time award winner of conspiracy theory fails: QAnon.

CHAPTER 9

QANON & THE 2020 PRESIDENTIAL ELECTION

The internet in general and social media specifically have changed the landscape of conspiracy theory from something that historically existed in small, isolated clusters of followers to a phenomenon that could gain an audience very quickly and spread globally within hours.

What came to be known as QAnon has its roots in many smaller threads of conspiracy theories that have been around for decades. In Chapter 11, we'll talk about the concept of the Deep State, which has been around in one form or another for hundreds of years and persists today a nearly omnipotent catchall bucket used by conspiracy theorists when a theory lacks tangible evidence or logical reasoning. It's a broad umbrella over the tapestry of conspiracies that came together online to form QAnon.

The Clintons have long been a target of propaganda and conspiracy theories dating back to the Whitewater investigation. Whitewater was a development investment deal the Clintons joined in the late 1970s that ultimately failed in the 1980s. It wasn't initially controversial until Bill Clinton ran for president in 1992, at which time it was conveniently brought to the forefront and spawned multiple investigations. Ultimately, several people involved in the deal were convicted of fraud and one of the main drivers behind the deal, James (Jim) McDougal, died in prison of a heart attack in 1998 during Bill Clinton's second presidential term. Multiple investigations confirmed the Clintons' financial interests but didn't find a connection between them and any of the fraud committed by other players. President Clinton himself initiated a federal investigation into Whitewater, which led to the Ken Starr investigation that ultimately revealed the president's affair with White House intern Monica Lewinsky. When Clinton lied about the affair under oath, it became the basis for the impeachment proceedings that dominated his second term in office.

It's not hard to see how the Clintons might encourage a thousand conspiracy theories associating them with secret crimes. The death of McDougal was the root of the later infamous "Hillary Hit List" of people the Clintons supposedly had killed in order to cover their crimes. (We'll cover that briefly in Chapter 11.)

Before we follow this path, let's take our project management approach and apply it to this first conspiracy: that the Clintons had McDougal killed in prison to shut him up. If the goal is to keep him from talking, does this achieve the goal? Yes, most definitely. Is it practical? No. He'd already gone through trial; he was already in prison. His death would raise suspicion. There would've been better opportunities before he was arrested if the plan was to cut off loose ends and his wife Susan McDougal would've been a target too. If the plan was to stop people from incriminating the Clintons, there were many better targets who'd have been eliminated much earlier, and by the time McDougal died, the issue was mostly over. In Chapter 11, I'll compare this with the conspiracy around Jeffrey Epstein's death in jail—a claim that makes more sense given that he died before any chance at a trial or conviction.

After the 1990s, the Clintons, specifically Hillary, became popular targets for conspiracy theories, including the one most relevant to this chapter and QAnon: Pizzagate.

Pizzagate didn't start with the anonymous individual or individuals known as "Q." It started on Twitter in October 2016, claiming that a certain interpretation of the leaked emails of former Clinton associates suggested a pedophile ring, known to the New York City Police Department, was being run by Democrats through a pizzeria in Washington, DC, specifically Comet Ping Pong pizzeria. Further details claimed the pedophile ring was being run out of the basement of the pizzeria despite the nagging detail that the building had no basement. Of course, this kind of structural detail doesn't stop conspiracy theorists. They simply claimed the basement was secret. It's not hard to imagine that with less than a month before the presidential election between Hillary Clinton and Donald Trump, this rumor would spread like wildfire across right-wing news outlets and propaganda sources. This got picked up by 4chan, an online message board that later became notorious as the birthplace of "Q." It's essentially a site where people can anonymously post about any topic.

And here we pause to talk about why "Q," when they appeared, wasn't unique. In fact, "Q" was a complete stereotype of the supposed individual with very high security clearance leaking information to the general public. Such characters have been around for a very long time. Even before technology brought them together and gave them an instant audience of millions, they were in bars and clubs claiming to be secret agents in order to impress people or get dates. In the 1994 movie *True Lies* with Bill Paxton, Arnold Schwarzenegger, and Jamie Lee Curtis, Paxton played such a character, trying to woo women with stories of being a spy and speaking in much of the same stereotypical language used on message boards. Although played for laughs, his character was a very accurate representation of people whose imitation of being "high security clearance and top secret" comes more from movies, TV, and books than from real life.

In conspiracy media, you'll frequently hear guests who have "secret insider information" and a high security clearance who want to remain anonymous for their own protection, but for some reason, they want to leak information to this specific media. Think about that for a moment. Does that make sense? You have secret information. Leaking it would be such a personal threat that you wish to remain anonymous, but you leak it to a source—a conspiracy theory site, podcast, or radio program—where few in the general population would believe you. You're not leaking the information to anyone who can do anything with the information and the only people who'll recognize it as true are the very people you want to hide from. Given that it's secret information, there are probably very few people who know about it, so it won't be hard for them to track down who's leaking the information and get rid of you. Because you chose to remain anonymous, your disappearance won't raise any suspicion. It really doesn't seem like the right way to go about it, does it?

Have there been secret informants who leaked important or secret information and wished to remain anonymous? Yes. There's a precedent in the real world that can explain the willingness of conspiracy theorists to believe in other secret leaks. Probably the most famous of these is associated with the Watergate scandal, which I mentioned very early in the book. An informant who went by the name "Deep Throat" (later revealed to be associate FBI director Mark Felt) leaked vital information to two reporters who were investigating the case.

And right there I gave you a clue to the biggest difference between a real anonymous informant and a fictional one. Did you spot it? A real informant will leak the information to someone who can do something with it—the mass media or law enforcement.

Of course, the safest route if you want to leak important information is to go completely public with it. Dump all the information to the mass media, law enforcement, or the general public and come forward personally to verify your identify, credentials, and access to the information. Think about Edward Snowden, who in 2013 leaked highly classified information from the National Security Agency (NSA) regarding surveillance operations around the globe by various governments as well as some private telecommunications companies. Snowden had worked as a contractor for the NSA and CIA. Without him coming forward, it would've been easy to disregard the information he exposed as fictional. To be believed, it needed a credible, verified source.

So back to "Q" and why the postings from "Q" look more like the postings of someone faking it rather than the postings of someone with a real security clearance. First, the posts are unnecessarily short and coded—exactly the kind of language used by someone whose idea of top secret operations comes from movies and TV, not from working in a genuine high-security job. Second, the postings were on a board where the posters are anonymous, so the information can be easily discarded and the user base doesn't include anyone who'd benefit in any way from the information or be in a position to do anything about it.

For example, one of the first posts by "Q" appeared on 4chan in October 2017 and predicted the imminent arrest of Hillary Clinton. Specifically, the post said: "HRC extradition already in motion effective yesterday with several countries in case of cross border run. Passport approved to be flagged effective 10/30 @ 12:01am. Expect massive riots organized in defiance and others fleeing the US to occur. US M's [military] will conduct the operation while NG [National Guard] activated."

Of course, the predicted event didn't happen, so it was followed by an even more obscure post: "Mockingbird HRC detained, not arrested (yet). Where is Huma? Follow Huma. This has nothing to do w/ Russia (yet). Why does Potus surround himself w/ generals? What is military intelligence?" And still more ramblings followed that come across more as a stream-of-consciousness word salad than any information coming from someone with inside information and high-security access. It sounds like the fan-fiction version of a spy novel.

As time went on and "Q" moved from 4chan to 8chan (because 4chan had supposedly been "infiltrated," but I guess 8chan was safe), followed by several more moves. The messages became more stereotypical—"The storm is coming, the destruction of the global cabal is imminent, follow the money"—and more obscure, such as "Find the reflection in the castle." And, of course, the ultimate backpedal: "Some things must remain classified to the very end." Ultimately, of all the "Q" claims and predictions, not a single one has ended up happening or shown to be correct.

A father–son team from Arizona is often pegged as the actual source of "Q" posts, but there's no doubt that the transition of "Q" posts from obscure message boards into broader media was initiated by others seeking to profit from the followers. The most obvious and extreme evidence of profiteering from "Q" followers was in 2021, when an individual who didn't claim to be "Q" but posted on "Q-"associated boards suggested that John F. Kennedy Jr., son of assassinated president John F. Kennedy, wasn't actually dead. (JFK Jr. died in a plane crash off the East Coast of the US in 1999.) Q claimed JFK Jr. would reappear at Dealey Plaza in Dallas (the site of JFK's assassination) and announce the reinstatement of Donald Trump as president and himself as vice president. Not only did people appear at Dealey Plaza expecting this to happen, but many people gave money to the person who originated the rumor— in some cases, their life savings—and stayed in Dallas for several months waiting for the event to occur. By no surprise, the deceased JFK Jr. never appeared.

"Q" came to be known as QAnon because they remained anonymous, spawning multiple rumors and side conspiracies of who it might be but also opening the door for anyone to step in and claim to be "Q." Contrary to what some people believe, the writings of "Q" don't have a unique or specific pattern. The stream-of-consciousness and sometimes word salad form of writing is very easy to duplicate.

How does the concept of "Q" as a real person with a high security clearance fit into our model? Poorly. First, the supposed first post by "Q" suggests Hillary Clinton was about to be arrested. What's the goal of leaking that information? There'd be no point in leaking the information. It doesn't alert anyone to secret operations and it's not being released in a location where anyone could do anything with the information or benefit from it. It's not worth taking a chance of exposing yourself simply to leak it.

If "Q" was or is fake, do the posts make sense? Yes. If the goal is simply clickbait to draw attention and potentially make money, such posts achieve that goal. They draw attention from a group of followers who'll be attracted to any information that fits their pre-existing beliefs and political biases. Keeping the identity of "Q" a secret also opens the door for anyone to take on that role for their own purposes.

Think of QAnon as a net thrown over the conspiracy theory community to pull together people who had believed in multiple individual conspiracies over time, (such as a global cabal of child sex predators or Hillary Clinton, Barack Obama, or James Comey being investigated and about to be arrested.

Does QAnon count as what we'd call a cult? In Chapter 8, I mentioned that what we think of as a cult and brainwashing comes out of the 1950s and 1960s and simply applies to views that are beyond the socialized norms of the culture as well as groups that attach very powerfully and emotionally to the views of the institution. But there are some traits of these groups that make them more likely to be viewed by a large percentage of the general population as "cults." The biggest is the degree of threat they represent either immediately or potentially to the followers. Any church could be seen by people outside the church as a cult, but most churches don't represent imminent risk to the followers. However, a small religious group that adheres to an end-of-the-world view can be a threat if the members are forgoing future plans, selling assets, and giving away financial resources to the leaders of the group.

The JFK Jr. believers in Dallas fit this criterion because there were several who liquidated resources and, in some cases, spent savings to travel to Dallas or to donate to the individual who started the rumor in the belief the claim was true. So in this sense, QAnon fits the criteria as a cult, but they miss it in one key area: There's no singular leader. As I mentioned, "Q" is anonymous and likely multiple people have made posts claiming to be "Q." Even people who don't claim to be "Q" have posted on the message boards and influenced followers toward specific beliefs and conspiracies. This is key to our next section.

The 2020 Presidential Election and Claims of Voter Fraud

If you weren't paying attention to politics between 2016 and 2020, this one might have caught you off guard. Otherwise, it not only was *not* a surprise, but you expected it.

We'll start with the event. The 2020 presidential election pitted incumbent Republican Donald Trump against Democratic challenger Joe Biden, former senator and then vice president under Barack Obama from 2008 to 2016. Pre-election polls had the race close, but most were indicating a lead for Biden. Election night played to a slower-than-usual timeline because of the COVID-19 pandemic, which caused a larger number of voters to vote by mail rather than in person and had caused several states without a widespread vote-by-mail system to hurry a system into place for voter safety. The Democrats supported this. The Republicans were against it and voiced suspicion of the security of the vote-by-mail system even though several states had been entirely vote-by-mail for several years without problems.

We need to take a brief sidestep into political psychology for a moment to understand why the parties would have different attitudes toward an expanded vote-by-mail system in this election. Historically, Republicans are very consistent in turning out in good numbers for presidential elections—whether they like the candidate their party put on the ticket or not. On the other hand, Democrats tend to be more idealistic in their choices and are more likely to vote third party or not at all if the Democratic Party doesn't put its preferred candidate on the final ballot. This was obvious in the 2000 presidential election when Ralph Nader split a small percentage of the Democratic vote away from

Al Gore and in 2016 when a percentage of Bernie Sanders supporters refused to support Hillary Clinton. Less common for the Republicans was Ross Perot pulling votes away from the re-election of George H.W. Bush in 1992.

Democrats tend to be less consistent in turning out to vote overall. If an election features a widely popular Democratic candidate or a widely unpopular Republican candidate, Democrats will turn out in large numbers, but otherwise, it can be difficult to get a large turnout. In states that have shifted to voting by mail, Democrats vote in more consistent numbers, attributed to the added convenience of voting early without the need to stand in line or be forced to vote within a certain time frame on a single day.

It was predicted that increasing voting by mail nationally because of the pandemic would increase the number of Democrats turning out to vote, so it's not hard to understand why Democrats would publicly support the move while Republicans would resist it.

So why did a more widespread vote-by-mail system change the timeline on election night? Because many states didn't start counting the mail-in ballots until the polls closed in those states. This caused a delay in those results being displayed. As predicted, in-person voting numbers heavily skewed Republican, while the mail-in results heavily skewed Democrat. It wasn't surprising (even predicted by many election night analysts as the night wore on) that vote totals would initially be heavily Republican and then start shifting more toward Democrats as the mail-ins were counted. This caused some people to believe that the early ballot counts, which in many cases favored Republicans, were genuine but that the later ballot counts, favoring Democrats, were fake.

The roots of 2020 election fraud conspiracies started in 2016 when the polls were leaning toward Hillary Clinton winning the election. Donald Trump stated before the election that it was rigged. This wasn't new. Conspiracy theorists have long claimed that the "global elite" decide the outcome of elections long before election days. Of course, in any given election year, this conspiracy would be most embraced by members of the party that lost the election. Why, in recent years, has this conspiracy become so pronounced and so emotionally supported?

Internet message boards in general and social media specifically are big drivers in laying the foundation for this belief. Why? Because we can self-select what sources we're exposed to. Quite often, those sources support our existing beliefs. If you support a particular candidate, you're likely to surround yourself with people and selective media that also support that candidate. This causes the "false consensus effect," in which you feel your beliefs are more common among the general population than they are. It makes sense that you'd feel overconfident that your candidate will win and, therefore, surprised, shocked, and disappointed when they lose. It's not hard to see you'd also be very willing to believe claims that the election was stolen in some way, even if the proposed mechanism or method of the steal doesn't make practical sense.

Right from the start, our project management approach makes this difficult—but not impossible—in a close election. Is it rational and viable to make the attempt in the first place? Yes and no. Yes, because it's happened in the past. No, because there are greater safeguards in place today than ever before. In the 18th and 19th centuries in the United States, voter fraud and manipulation were quite common but only in local and state races. There were no known attempts to influence a national election because it would involve too many people organized across too many states. It would have to work perfectly to not be exposed.

Why was manipulation in local and state elections so common in the past? For many reasons. Not all communities had directories of the local population; therefore, someone could stuff ballot boxes with enough votes to throw an election. Illiteracy was so common that "voice voting" was allowed in many communities where someone would simply say who they were voting for and someone else would write it down.

Even in the 20th century, when it became more common to verify registered voters, assign them specific voting locations, and have them sign logs when they showed up to vote, volunteers could still stuff ballot boxes after the polls closed. It was simple and common in influencing local races. The workers had access to the logs showing who did and didn't show up to vote and could simply start signing names and stuffing ballots. It would likely only be discovered if a recount was ordered or if a precinct had a suspiciously high voter turnout compared with other nearby precincts. In fact, fraud at in-person voting sites was part of the motivation for making elections more secure by using mail-in ballots in which no one could see who you voted for until the ballot reached its final destination.

If you were going to attempt to influence the outcome of a national election, how might you do it? You'd want to insert as few ballots as possible to limit the chance they'll be detected, which means you won't make any attempts in states where a candidate has a large lead in the polls. You'll focus on states where your candidate is trailing but within the margin of error.

What's the margin of error? It's the "plus or minus" points mentioned when giving poll results, such as "Candidate X is leading by 3 points, plus or minus 5 points." If the plus or minus is greater than the candidate's lead, it's simply a prediction that the eventual winner is predicted to be within that margin, and even though one candidate is leading, it wouldn't be statistically unusual for the other candidate to end up winning. This means trying to swing the vote artificially wouldn't raise suspicion because it would still be a statistically likely outcome.

So we focus on close states and target the larger communities where we could insert more votes and hope no one notices. Does this plan have a chance to achieve the goal? Yes. Is it a rational plan? Only if the focus is a local race where the number of votes needed is very small.

Why is it not rational on a national level? Because there are too many checks and balances in place monitoring elections. This isn't the 18th or 19th century anymore. People register to vote and signatures are kept on file, but there are people in every election who try to vote more than once (such as being registered in two districts or asking for a mail-in ballot but then also showing up to vote at a polling place) and people who submit votes for dead relatives. These anomalies are easily detected and corrected. Also in Michigan, a live tabulation map displayed a sudden jump of more than 100,000 votes for Biden but none for Trump. This wasn't an error in the actual votes being counted; it was an error by the people running the election monitoring website where the map was displayed. The map was quickly updated to include the updated totals for Trump. Human error had caused several thousand votes to be incorrectly logged for Biden in Antrim County, Michigan. Within hours, it was discovered and corrected.

After all results were counted in the 2020 election, Joe Biden had approximately 7 million more votes than Donald Trump. Could 7 million votes be inserted secretly and not be discovered? Not a chance. This is demonstrated by recounts in multiple states, where in some cases, machine counts were double-checked by hand.

The frequent argument is: "They were all in on it, even some Republican election officials." If such a widespread conspiracy were possible by the one party, Hillary Clinton would've easily won in 2016. Trump's margin of victory in some states in 2016 was very small. If a party can sneak in more than 7 million votes, it should be simple to run through tens of thousands undetected.

The "stolen election" conspiracy violates our criteria in multiple ways:

- It would take too many people.
- It would involve too many materials.
- It must be so precisely faked that phony ballots look identical to real ballots.
- The vote counts can't exceed the number of registered voters in that area.
- Any fraudulent manipulation of voting machines would be easily discovered by hand recounts of the physical ballots.
- The consequences of being discovered would be tremendous. Better to risk losing one election than to take the chance your party will be forever tainted and have trouble winning any election.

There's another big problem with the claims of the 2020 election results being fake. What about the other races on the same ballot? You'd need thousands of variations of fake ballots and data manipulation to cover the variety of down-ballot races in different districts. You'd have to be extremely careful not to mix any of these into the wrong districts where they'd be easily discovered. Possibly most important, anyone who paid attention in civics knows control of Congress is more important than the presidency. If Democrats had the people and materials necessary to fake an election by more than 7 million votes completely undetected, they'd have also won a substantial majority in the House of Representatives and Senate. There'd never have been a runoff election in Georgia and the Democrats wouldn't have simply squeaked out a tie in the Senate.

What about videos of vans behind precincts unloading tubs or a tub being pulled out from under a table at an election facility during the count? Well—what about it? It tells us nothing about what was in the tubs. Could have been more legal ballots from late-reporting precincts, could have been empty tubs for storing counted ballots, could have been soft drinks for election workers.

What about "all the evidence"? If I've not angered one side of the political spectrum yet, this will probably do it. There was no evidence. None. There were claims of evidence by people with personal investment in the outcome and by people seeking attention for personal gain or profit, but this evidence was never revealed or turned over to anyone who could do anything about it.

Earlier, I mentioned that people with a high security clearance who want to leak information to the public aren't going to leak it to obscure outlets where nothing can be done with it. They'll release it to the mass media or authorities. The same applies to the claims of evidence in the 2020 election. Someone with actual evidence isn't going to go on national TV talking about the supposed evidence. Instead, they'll deliver the evidence to authorities, then talk about it later.

In other conspiracies, I talk about better options for achieving the same goal without needing as many people, with less chance of being discovered, and with greater chance of success. In this case, there's no option that has any chance of success without being uncovered. As much as some don't want to admit it, our elections have become about as secure as we can make them. The fact that even small cases of voter fraud—sometimes a handful or a couple dozen fraudulent ballots out of tens of thousands can be discovered and corrected—tells us there'd be no way to fake hundreds of thousands and especially not millions of votes. This conspiracy is and was dead on arrival.

Before leaving this one, there's an equal and opposite conspiracy theory that suffers from all the same problems. This one suggests that Donald Trump assumed his loss was because of fraud and fake ballots because he'd masterminded a similar operation in order to win the election in 2016 and arranged for more fake ballots in the 2020 election so he'd have more votes than Hillary Clinton had in 2016. In a nutshell, he quickly accused the Democrats of fraud and fake ballots because he was using fraud and fake ballots himself. Supporters of this conspiracy note that in the fallout of the 2020 election and the demand for recounts, Republicans refused recount requests in states where Trump had won. As I mentioned earlier, in the 2016 election, Trump won several states, such as Michigan, by quite narrow margins. Therefore, it would take fewer fake votes to swing a couple key states his direction, but we're still talking about votes in the thousands or tens of thousands in a system where we easily uncover mere dozens of fraudulent votes. So this counterconspiracy, like the other, is dead on arrival and sits on the irrational end of our conspiracy spectrum.

Voter fraud to swing a couple dozen votes in a local race? Rational and possible. Fraud on a national scale? Sorry. The infrastructure doesn't exist to pull it off undetected no matter how many people are in on it.

CHAPTER 10

COVID-19 & THE COVID VACCINES

Much like the 9/11 attacks on the United States in 2001, the number and variety of conspiracy theories surrounding COVID-19 and the later vaccines could fill their own book. We'll address a few of the specific theories, but more generally, we'll look at categories of theories and the validity of some of the key claims.

Let's start with what COVID-19 is, what the term means, and where it comes from. That itself is a root to most of the confusion—misunderstanding and misinformation that fueled many of the early conspiracy theories. COVID-19 stands for *Corona* (CO) *Virus* (VI) *Disease* (D) and *19* represents the year it was first identified (2019). It's the name of the disease you get from the virus. The specific virus is SARS-CoV 2 (severe acute respiratory syndrome coronavirus 2). "Coronavirus" as a general term refers to a group of viruses that are part of the broader *Coronaviridae* family of viruses, many of which, along with rhinovirus, produce what we think of as the common cold.

Some of the coronaviruses cause much more severe infections than the common cold and are much more likely to cause long-term effects or death. SARS (severe acute respiratory syndrome, first reported in China in 2002) and MERS (Middle East respiratory syndrome, first reported in Saudi Arabia in 2012) are also part of this family. So simply referring to COVID-19 as *the* coronavirus isn't accurate and can be dangerously confusing. For example, when a bottle of disinfectant spray says it kills coronavirus, it's probably referring to the milder strains, not to SARS-CoV-2. You can see why people who think all coronaviruses are the same would be easily convinced that the media attention around COVID-19 is exaggerated.

In December 2019, SARS-CoV-2 was first identified in Wuhan, China, as the cause of what was being reported as a very severe pneumonia that spread quickly throughout the population. China locked down much of the city to limit the spread and informed the World Health Organization (WHO) of the new strain, but by this time, it had already spread outside the community. Thanks to global air travel, it was spreading to other countries.

A phylogenetic algorithm studying the timeline of the spread suggests the virus was probably spreading as early as October or November 2019 before it was finally identified as a new strain and it might have been appearing in Guangdong, China, before it appeared in Wuhan. The animal market in Wuhan, which was an early focus as the origin of the virus via a live animal market, might have been a super-spreader event and not the original source. This is very possible given that a new strain is unlikely to be identified immediately and will have plenty of time to spread before it's identified.

By March 2020, Italy had overtaken China with the most COVID-19 deaths, and by late March, the United States surpassed Italy and China in the number of confirmed cases. By late March 2020, the United States had implemented a COVID-19 shutdown, with many schools and businesses closing to limit the spread and prevent hospitals from being overrun with COVID-19 patients. Obviously, this created immediate economic hardship for millions of people.

By December 2020, the first vaccines became available to the public, but there were concerns that the vaccines wouldn't maintain long-term effectiveness and might require booster shots. By September 2021, the US Food and Drug Administration (FDA) began approving an additional vaccine dose (booster) for vulnerable populations six months after receiving their last dose, and a few months later, booster shots were recommended for all adults.

What fueled COVID-19 conspiracies early in the pandemic was the politicizing of the illness. Between the first confirmed case in the United States on January 20th and the shutdowns in March, there was a lot of criticism of the Trump administration's response to the pandemic, with administration supporters claiming the threat was being exaggerated in order to make the president look bad.

This is where things get wacky and weird. Not only was there a spread of multiple conspiracies, but many people supported completely contradictory theories, such as COVID-19 itself being a hoax while simultaneously saying it was a bioweapon launched by China. I'll address these two theories independently because they tend to be the foundation for many other conspiracies. There's no point addressing others if the root to the theory doesn't hold up.

COVID-19 Is a Hoax

This one mostly originated in the United States early in the pandemic, specifically claiming the Democratic Party was using a hoax virus to make Donald Trump look bad and help the Democrats win the 2020 presidential election.

Some claimed the virus would magically disappear after the election. Obviously, it didn't go away after the election, so the conspiracy evolved more broadly to the government trying to control people by taking away their rights. This broader form of the conspiracy didn't stay limited to the United States; it quickly spread to any country imposing COVID-related shutdowns and restrictions.

We only need to address one of our criteria to put this conspiracy on the irrational side of the spectrum: How many people would it take to carry out and maintain this conspiracy? As of January 2022, only two countries in the world were confirmed to have experienced no COVID cases during the pandemic: Tuvalu and Nauru. Both are isolated island countries with traditionally low traffic from other countries. North Korea and Turkmenistan also claimed to have no cases, but given the nature of their governments, their ease of controlling internal media, and their global locations, it's unlikely they truly had no cases. This means every country in the world except those mentioned would have to be in on the conspiracy and all of them would have to agree to keep it secret.

Can you think of any time in modern history where we could expect every country in the world to agree on anything? In fact, it would be a very powerful political win for a country to expose the hoax to the world. This is a major problem with any conspiracy that would require a large number of people or groups to participate and keep the secret: There's plenty of power and advantage to being the one who exposes it to the world. We mentioned this earlier with the moon landing hoax: The Soviet Union would've been the first to expose it and grab the opportunity to humiliate the United States globally. There's no way they'd have participated in the cover-up.

The other problem with the COVID-19 hoax conspiracy is the goal. If it's to exert more control over people of a nation/jurisdiction, what sort of control would this virus/infection/danger give the governmental body it doesn't already possesses? In the United States, you're registered and cataloged with a Social Security number; you need a driver's license to drive; you must register your vehicle to drive it and pay fees every year to continue using it; you need a fishing license to fish and a hunting license to hunt; in many areas, you must register to carry a weapon; the property you think you own is actually leased from the government in the form of property taxes that must be paid or the government will take your property; and if you want to do any major improvements to your property, you must get permits. What sort of extra control would such a massive global conspiracy give them that they don't already have? And would such additional control be worth the complexity and risk of putting together a global cover-up?

Governments already have three historically effective methods for control: media, religion, and nationalism. Use those three and nothing else is necessary. All three are already very well rooted in every country.

All this puts the hoax conspiracy well down on the irrational side of the spectrum, but let's address why so many people could be led to believe it. COVID-19 shutdowns in any country put tremendous stress on the citizens—sometimes simply the psychological stress of being socially limited in movement and isolated from your social circles and also the financial stress of not being able to work and therefore struggling to pay basic bills. It's no surprise such stress would lead to venting on the institutions ordering and enforcing the shutdowns. People participating in the early COVID-19 shutdown protests in the United States voiced frustrations about not being able to eat out, get a haircut, go to the bar, or go bowling. These weren't concerns about financial health but about simple freedom of movement and freedom to do what they want and go where they want. Hence, the focus is on "losing freedom." It's no surprise that mask mandates were then labeled by some as "muzzling" and a further attempt to take away rights. In fact, the images in the media of middle- and lower-middle-class white people claiming their rights were being violated because they weren't free to do rather mundane things added fuel to the pressure cooker that went off several months later when George Floyd was killed in Minneapolis.

COVID Is a Bioweapon Released by China

This has its roots in Wuhan, China, being the first reported outbreak of COVID-19 and in Wuhan being the location of a coronavirus research facility. It seemed like an incredible coincidence. But was it? Not at all. As mentioned at the beginning of this chapter, it's now thought the virus was spreading in other communities before it reached Wuhan. Why would it be identified as a new strain in Wuhan? Because there was a coronavirus research facility there with the necessary technology to identify the virus and recognize it as a new strain. It's no coincidence at all that the virus would spread until it reached a community with the facilities to identify it. What about the specific theory that the virus was being developed as a biological weapon and was accidentally released from the facility? Would that be a rational conspiracy? Maybe, but there are several problems:

- Viruses are poor choices for bioweapons because of the limited ability to control their spread.
- Because of the control China has over its people and media, it would've been very easy to cover up the

outbreak until it was first reported in another country, thereby taking the focus off them as an origin point.
- If you were developing a biological weapon and released it either intentionally or accidentally, you wouldn't be the first to report it to the WHO.

If we put ourselves inside a secret dark-ops group given the task of developing and spreading a new biological weapon, there's no situation in which we'd release it in our own country first or, in the case of an accidental release, allow it to be identified within our own country. It's easier and safer to wait until other countries have noticed this new "severe pneumonia" and had their own facilities identify it as a new strain. By that time, the spread would be wide enough that it would be very difficult to pin its origin to our country.

Does this mean it could still be a biological weapon, originating from another country and first released in China to point the finger at them? Maybe. But unlikely because of the first bullet point mentioned. In our current world of international air travel, a virus as contagious as COVID-19 wouldn't be considered a viable biological weapon because of the inability to control the spread. This is why *Bacillus anthracis* (anthrax) makes an ideal biological weapon. It's fatal, can be precisely targeted in an easy-to-control yet hard-to-detect way, and isn't contagious in the way viruses are contagious. However, there's one popular conspiracy theory that doesn't care if a virus is hard to control. In fact, it depends on it.

COVID-19 Is a Biological Weapon Meant to Reduce World Population

The idea of a global elite wanting to kill off large numbers of people for various reasons has been around a long time and covers everything from 5G technology to fluoride in drinking water, chemtrails, vaccines, and food additives, so it's no surprise COVID-19 conspiracies would also jump on this bandwagon. If the goal is to reduce world population, how does this fit our criteria?

- A virus with the fatality rate of COVID-19 achieves the goal of reducing the population without causing global extinction.
- It wouldn't require very many people—only a select group who organized the initial release of the virus. Even the people who developed the virus wouldn't need to know the purpose of the virus or be aware it had been released.
- The risk of being discovered is low, and even if the plan is uncovered, it would be easy to explain it away as a mutated virus that accidentally escaped a lab without anyone being aware.
- It's hard to imagine a better way to achieve the goal without involving more people and a higher risk of being discovered.

Seems like this one should be high on the rational and possible end of the spectrum, doesn't it? As you can guess, it has a big plot hole: What would be the reason for wanting to kill millions of people? "The elite want to thin the population" conspiracy theories, regardless of the focus, have this same problem. What's the benefit to the elite of reducing the population?

Many suggest that the desire to reduce the world population has to do with reducing the consumption of resources—the belief we're populating ourselves off the planet and that as more people compete for fewer resources, wars will break out, economies will collapse, and, of course, the elite will have their power and wealth threatened.

Others claim the goal is to get rid of the starving, poor, and unemployed because they're a burden on the system.

There's a flaw here that's common in many conspiracy theories: Start with an assumption as fact, then base the rest of the conspiracy on that assumption. That's fine if the assumption is true, but the entire conspiracy falls apart if the assumption is false.

As of 2020, the global population was estimated to be around 7.7 billion people. In 1950, it was 2.5 billion. But guess what? In the 1950s, people already believed in conspiracies about the global elite wanting to thin out the population for all the same reasons mentioned above. Two world wars and the 1918 influenza pandemic (also known as the Spanish flu pandemic) didn't prevent the global population from increasing from 2 billion in 1900 to 2.5 billion in 1950.

Why the fear of overpopulation? The first thing that comes to mind is the inability to feed everyone. Are we at a point right now where that's an issue? Are so many people starving because of the size of the population? People were also starving in 1900 and 1950.

People aren't starving because of the size of the population; they're starving because of the distribution infrastructure of resources. In advanced countries, the poor and unemployed might be a financial burden on government aid and social programs, but it wouldn't be a problem for the rich and powerful global elite. In fact, the global elite require a certain percentage of the population to be unemployed and struggling because that makes workers compete for jobs rather than having companies competing for workers. This helps businesses keep wages relatively low. Obviously, that benefits the wealthy and powerful.

The other problem with reducing population is that the population is on the cusp of doing that by itself. The global birth rate has been steadily dropping for more than a half century. It's dropped by half since 1950. There does seem to be a point where human population will reach a maximum—some suggest around 9.5 billion by the 2060s—then start to decline until reaching a stable point, possibly around 8 billion by the end of the century. Of course, that's not considering potential global wars or devastating plagues, which would obviously drop the population much more.

In addition, look at the result of COVID-19 from 2020 into 2022. The economy rebounded, but the workforce didn't. Some workers died; some COVID-19 long-haulers hadn't fully recovered and hadn't been able to return to the workforce; some two-income families adapted to one income as a partner either temporarily or permanently left the workforce; there was a jump in the number of baby boomers choosing to retire; and many others chose changes in career paths as the shutdowns demonstrated that remote work was not only viable but in many cases also more productive than in-person work. Many people abandoned low-paying food service jobs, forcing companies in those industries to offer higher wages to attract workers back. And, of course, the powerful global elite don't like paying higher wages—at least not to the average worker.

By the numbers, the idea that the elite would benefit from reducing the population doesn't pan out. They benefit from a larger population because it means more workers and more consumers, and without those, the elite have no wealth or power.

Within our conspiracy theory criteria, a virus to kill a limited percentage of the population is viable. It fits on the more plausible side of our spectrum, but the practical reason for it makes no sense, the application would likely have the opposite of the desired effect, and the potential risk if it was discovered would be tremendous: charges of attempted genocide. This sets us up for the last section.

COVID-19 Vaccine Conspiracies

The anti-vax movement has a long history of conspiracy theories, but the specific ones around the COVID-19 vaccines were fueled—much like the COVID-19 hoax ones—by the unfortunate politicization of COVID-19, especially in the United States.

There are three broad conspiracies here:

- The vaccine does nothing; it's simply meant to reinforce the COVID-19 hoax.
- The vaccine was rushed and data was faked; therefore, it's dangerous.
- The vaccine is meant to track or kill millions of people.

There's also a counterconspiracy to these that I'll mention near the end of this chapter.

We need to start with the broad vaccine conspiracies: the anti-vax movement supported long before COVID-19 because the COVID-19 vaccine conspiracies share many of these characteristics as well as many of the flaws.

Vaccines Are a Tool by Big Pharma to Make Money

There are two general parts to this one: Vaccines do nothing (they're pushed for profit) and vaccines cause disease (so the medical industry can make money treating them). There's a related conspiracy theory that—depending on how it's applied—can be contradictory to the others: Big Pharma has a cure for cancer but won't release it because there's too much money to be made treating cancer and raising money for cancer research.

It's true that if there were a vaccine to prevent cancer, it would be much cheaper than cancer treatment. But there's a trade-off between losing the thousands of people who wouldn't need cancer treatment versus selling a vaccine to hundreds of millions of people. There's a huge flaw in almost all vaccine conspiracy theories—and it's the most common flaw in all the conspiracies we've covered: It would involve too many people. Conspiracists claim most of the medical field is in on it—from the researchers and labs to your neighborhood doctor. They're all in on it—all keeping it secret in exchange for kickbacks from the industry.

But let's back up and look at where these conspiracies would fall on our spectrum and within the project management approach. Would it be practical to sell a remedy that doesn't work in order to make money? Yes. Research and development would be very cheap if you don't care if it works. There's definitely a market of people with various illnesses looking for treatments and cures, and within a single pharmaceutical company, it wouldn't involve very many people if you're limiting the number of people who know the drug doesn't work but convincing the rest of your employees it does work. History is filled with snake oil salesmen making a quick buck from fake remedies and those types of con artists are still around today, flourishing within the framework of alternative medicine, where there's no testing or oversight to verify their products work.

This is where we present an alternative conspiracy theory: The anti-vaccine movement was started and is promoted by the alternative medicine industry to drive people away from effective medications and treatments in order to boost their own sales. This one would also fit within the project management approach as a good plan. Only executives and the people producing the materials would need to know it's fake and it definitely wouldn't be hard to hire a handful of actors to offer anecdotal stories of the effectiveness.

We have a tale of two cautions. Does the pharmaceutical industry want you purchasing drugs you don't need so they can make money? They're private, profit-driven companies looking to expand their markets, so of course they want as many customers as possible. But alternative medicine is also privately owned and profit-driven and wants people buying products and treatments they don't need. The difference is the pharmaceutical industry has regulations governing them, requiring them to show proof their drugs or treatments work and are safe. Because alternative medicine isn't actually "medicine" by governmental standards, they don't have the same regulatory restrictions or requirement of efficacy. They can buy bulk green tea by the ton and break it down into little packages, selling it for $20 an ounce and claiming it's "super green tea." They can buy truckloads of mineral oil, add color and scent, and then bottle them as "essential oils" and get away with it as long as there's a disclaimer on their website that reads "supplier may substitute products."

The "Vaccines don't work" and "Vaccines cause disease" theories have another critical flaw that would need too many people to cover up: statistics. If vaccines didn't work, then the rate of disease would stay the same as the vaccine was distributed. If vaccines cause disease, then as millions of people get vaccinated, the rate of disease should increase accordingly. Decades of statistics show the very opposite. The higher the rate of vaccination within a population, the lower the rate of disease—and it's a very strong correlation.

In 1998, Andrew Wakefield's paper (since retracted), which claimed the MMR (measles, mumps, and rubella) vaccine causes autism, set off a wave of vaccine fear. It started an unfortunate drop in the number of people receiving the MMR vaccine. If Wakefield was correct and the vaccine was associated with autism, then as fewer people received the vaccine, the rate of autism should have slowed or declined. It didn't. It continued rising at the same rate.

Again, supporters of these conspiracies will claim data are faked and that doctors are misdiagnosing or, in the case of vaccines, causing diseases, not documenting these diseases. As I mentioned earlier, it's a cover-up that would involve almost the entire medical field. It would seem the cost of paying off tens of thousands of professionals to keep quiet would cut deeply into whatever profit was being made from the vaccines or the resulting illnesses.

In a nutshell, it would be a practical plan to increase profit, but the regulations and controls over the industry make it virtually impossible. Is it possible to fake preliminary data and maybe pay off a few researchers to claim something works when it doesn't? Yes—and that has happened, but it almost always gets uncovered because once the medication is in production and given to a large sample of clients, the statistics reveal it doesn't work.

Despite doubters thinking Big Pharma is a collection of companies all working together to maintain a big cover-up, the reality is quite different. Pharmaceutical companies are competing to bring drugs to the market. They spend millions of dollars developing the drugs and there are billions of dollars in profits on the line if the drug works— and millions in losses if it doesn't. With that general conspiracy field laid out, let's address COVID-19 vaccines specifically.

The COVID Vaccines Were Rushed

Why do so many drugs take years to get through development and trials before being approved by the FDA? There are many factors involved—too many to cover them all here—but there were two big differences in the COVID-19 vaccines that aren't usually present in typical drug trials: The federal government suspended some typical restrictions and allowed for emergency use, and the number of people volunteering for human trials in just the first weeks was greater than what researchers usually get over a span of years. It takes a certain threshold of volunteers to produce enough data to adequately drive the statistics and for the FDA to be willing to look at it, and for most drugs, it takes years to get enough volunteers. In the first months of COVID-19 vaccine research, there were tens of thousands of people volunteering to participate. That influx, combined with the government easing restrictions, guaranteed the first COVID-19 vaccine would reach the general public remarkably fast. There was nothing unusual about it. Most drugs would get to market just as quickly if those same conditions were present with all of them.

The COVID Vaccine Doesn't Work

This one, of course, runs contrary to the conspiracy that COVID-19 itself is a hoax because this one assumes COVID-19 is real but that the vaccine does nothing to prevent it. It's being marketed either for profit or in support of any of the other vaccine conspiracies we're about to cover.

Again, statistics prove it does work, with vaccinated people being less likely to experience serious illness, be hospitalized, or die compared with unvaccinated people, but believers in the conspiracy think the statistics are being faked and medical records are being altered.

Would it be a rational plan to market a quickly developed drug that doesn't work simply to grab a quick profit? Yes. Internally, not very many people would need to know about it. But when it comes to faking statistical data from a variety of independent sources, it would require too many people all willing to cooperate and keep the secret without anyone coming forward to expose the hoax. Again, the problem with trying to fake an FDA-approved drug is all the safeguards put in place to make sure the drug is safe and significantly effective to warrant being released to the general public.

The COVID Vaccine Contains Tracking Chips

This one falls immediately on the irrational/impossible side of the spectrum because it relies on technology that at the moment is science fiction. It would require a tracking chip and a power source that could fit through the head of a needle undetected. If we had technology like that, it would be worth billions of dollars in consumer technology.

If the technology existed, would it be a viable plan to plant trackers in people through a vaccine? Here's where I'd present a question to the class: You want to track the population. Can you think of ways to do it that would be better than putting microscopic trackers in vaccines? Think of the people who are paranoid about getting vaccines because they think trackers might be in them.

If you're part of a secret government group assigned the task of planting trackers on people, how do you get the trackers into those people? Well, if you have trackers and power sources small enough to fit through the head of a needle, you can fit them into anything: driver's license or photo IDs, insurance cards, debit/credit cards. You don't need them in cell phones because those can already track you. Assuming the tiny power supplies have a limited life span, you'll want a delivery system more frequent than vaccines and something with broader access to the general population. Easy targets would be food additives and drinking water.

In a nutshell, even if you could deliver trackers through a vaccine, it's not the route you'd take. It would be inefficient and too limited.

The COVID Vaccine Is Killing People

This one hearkens back to the population control conspiracy theories but is also fueled by "The vaccine was rushed and is therefore dangerous" beliefs. Like all the others, this one fails in the number of people, including every doctor in the country who's diagnosed COVID-19, being in on the cover-up to falsify or hide records in return for whatever kickbacks they're supposedly getting from Big Pharma.

Let's address that point for a moment. I've talked about the risk to the groups running the conspiracy if it's revealed and whether the risk is worth it. Would it be worth whatever they might be getting from the conspiracists to take the chance as an individual doctor that your falsification or destruction of records will be discovered? Shouldn't we see social media flooded with tens of thousands of claims by family members of a loved one passing away after getting the vaccine? And what is it these doctors are being asked to do? Cover up deaths from the vaccine while at the same time pushing the vaccine on others? Does it seem plausible that the entire medical profession would be in on something like this and not a single doctor would come forward and reveal they were asked to do this?

So not only would this conspiracy involve too many people to be considered rational or possible, but the application of it is also irrational and impossible. A doctor somewhere would've gone to the media (real media, not "I heard from someone I know" rumor media) to blow this up and stop it. But there's one more theory we need to cover:

It's a counterconspiracy to these in that it's pointing the threat in a different direction.

COVID-19 and the Vaccines Are Meant to Identify Uncooperative People and Anti-Vaxxers

With this one, we venture back into two categories we've already dismissed: population control and viruses as viable biological weapons. So do we immediately dismiss this one? Not quite. It comes with a few twists that save it from the "impossible" side of the spectrum. We'll call it the "dictator motivation." But first, let's address the conspiracy itself.

According to this conspiracy, COVID-19 is real and the vaccines work—but the vaccine *boosters* aren't for COVID-19; they're to protect against a much more deadly manufactured virus that will be released next. The motivation is to use the COVID-19 pandemic to gauge who in the population will cooperate and do what they're told (get vaccinated) and who won't. Most people who accepted the initial vaccination will likely get the boosters, so by protecting them against the next virus, you're keeping the cooperative people safe while guaranteeing the deaths of the people who refused to cooperate.

This is different from simply killing people off for population control. This is targeting a specific group based on behavior and getting rid of them because their behavior is a threat to those in power. The use of a virus as a biological weapon is different in this case because you're developing and administering the cure before releasing the disease, therefore having a degree of control over the spread of the virus. You can see why this would be called the "dictator motivation"—whittle out the people who could be a problem and keep the ones who are likely to be obedient and loyal. Is this rational? Not really. Let's outline the problems:

- Given that the pandemic is global, as is the distribution of the vaccines and boosters, we must assume this is a global conspiracy; therefore, it would involve too many people and, most especially, too many opposing governments.
- You have to consider whether the chance of consolidating power in your country by getting rid of the opposition would be worth allowing your enemies to do the same.
- As of January 2022, slightly more than 50% of the global population are fully vaccinated. If we assume the goal is to kill the majority of the unvaccinated, such a sudden drop in population would destroy the economic and social infrastructures of every country in the world.
- You're gambling the social stability of your country on the ability of all other nations to keep a secret without anyone revealing it. If this plan is revealed, many countries would likely collapse into chaos and civil war. Keep in mind, just because half the population were compliant in getting the vaccines and the boosters doesn't mean they'd support a government that intentionally killed half the population.

Any population control or selective weeding-out conspiracy has the same flaws: It's inherently self-destructive and any perceived benefit is completely washed away by the likely negative outcomes. But there are many people who do believe in these conspiracies, so the next part addresses your biggest question.

What Motivates People to Believe These Kinds of Conspiracies?

Several factors. The biggest we've mentioned before—and it's worth repeating: fear. Fear is the single biggest tool in the toolbox of anyone trying to influence or manipulate. Make someone afraid of a person, group, or situation and you have a foot in the door toward manipulating their behavior, beliefs, and interpretation of situations.

Another factor is suspicion, especially suspicion of people who are wealthy or in positions of power. It's the assumption that the powerful always have nefarious intent to increase their power or wealth. Where does this suspicion come from? Has a wealthy person ever been caught in a plot to microchip citizens or carry out mass killings for population control or an attempt to collapse the economy for whatever reason? No. (Bill Gates has suggested microchips for medical information, but that doesn't quite fit population control or population thinning.)

But if we return to "cultivation theory"—the means by which fictional media gets into our heads and influences how we interpret the real world—it's not hard to see how the media depicting villains being evil just for the sake of being evil have put into our heads the idea that any multibillionaire is secretly the villain from a James Bond movie, looking to either take over the world or destroy it. (Admittedly, Jeff Bezos flying into space in his own rocket had a Bond villain vibe to it.)

There's a much simpler explanation for people who refuse to get a vaccine: Are they simply afraid of needles? To be honest, that's likely the number one reason no adult is willing to admit. Being afraid of getting shots is a "kid thing," right? It's called "trypanophobia," and in the United States alone, it affects roughly 50 million people, or approximately 15% of the population. As of January 2022, about 25% of the US population hadn't received even one vaccination.

When you consider the number of people who because of health reasons can't receive a vaccination even if they want one, you're left with needle-phobics as a likely majority of the remainder. And who wants to admit they refused a potentially life-saving medicine simply because they're afraid of the shot? It's much easier to seek out excuses that would seem rational if they were true and cling to those reasons regardless of the magnitude of countering information.

CHAPTER 11

THE DEEP STATE & SECRETLY MURDERED CELEBRITIES

The Deep State is a bucket of secrecy and seemingly limitless cultural and political power that theorists use as the default source of anything mysterious when they can't identify a more specific person or group as the root of their conspiracy. It's the Santa Claus of conspiracy theories.

More specific descriptions of the Deep State usually target secret societies. You've heard of at least one of these: the Illuminati. You've possibly heard of some of the others: the Knights Templar, the Freemasons, and Skull and Bones.

As with the other conspiracies we've covered in this book, conspiracies rarely emerge from nowhere. There's usually a real-world example of secret operations that were somehow exposed to fuel the belief in other similar conspiracies. It's no surprise that the existence of "secret societies" would open the door to suspicion of almost anything.

The Knights Templar is the oldest of these secret societies, having been formed about 900 years ago and existing for almost 200 years before being supposedly dissolved. It was at that point that the group was rumored to have continued as a secret society—so secret in fact that there's no viable evidence they continued to exist. Of course, lack of evidence doesn't stop a conspiracy theory. It also helped promote conspiracies because they were very wealthy and powerful when they were "dissolved." Having started as a group of warriors meant to protect Christian pilgrims in the Holy Land during the Crusades, they later turned to banking. They owned an island and their own fleet of ships and army, and they loaned money to kings. It was when they refused loans to the king of France that things went bad for them. They were hunted, arrested, tortured, and killed. In 1312, Pope Clement V formally dissolved them and then confiscated and redistributed their wealth.

It's no surprise that a group so powerful would be suspected of continuing in secret and having the resources to keep the secret so they could continue influencing powerful people. Their symbol was the Cross of Lorraine, better known as the Jerusalem Cross, which isn't rare to see, but because it was the Knights Templar symbol, people believe any image of the symbol is a secret sign of the Knights Templar. Some people believe variations of the symbol are stamped on Oreo cookies and present in the logo of Nabisco.

There are some small groups who consider themselves Knights Templar today, but there's no indication the original powerful group still exists or that these small groups have any connection to the original.

What about the Freemasons? If you've not heard of them before, maybe you've heard of one of their subsets: the Shriners. Freemasons essentially started as a labor group in the Middle Ages. They were craftsmen who adopted an identifying symbol to recognize each other as they traveled. They're not a religion or a religious cult as some believe, but as time went on, they did adopt a spiritual element, recognizing a "Grand Architect of the Universe" and historically being involved with building cathedrals.

A third of the Founding Fathers who signed the US Constitution were Freemasons. They do have secret procedures and rituals, and their gathering place is called a "Masonic temple"—all lending an air of mystery around them and therefore making them fertile ground for conspiracy theories.

Probably the most well known of secret societies is the Illuminati. Formed in Bavaria in 1776 by Adam Weishaupt, they were intended to be an alternative to organized religion, basing beliefs and knowledge on reason rather than faith. Weishaupt recruited heavily from the Freemasons, looking to attract wealthy and powerful people into his new society. The Illuminati has been ripe for secrecy and conspiracy theories from the very beginning because they assigned their members nicknames and communicated in cipher. It took just more than a decade for them to be deemed illegal and stamped out, but like all the other secret societies, their end didn't stop the belief that they continued in secrecy, led by the rich and powerful, influencing world events behind the scenes. Of all the secret societies I mention here, the Illuminati has been represented the most in fiction, especially movies, when filmmakers want to reference a secret society influencing major events.

One "secret society" you might not have heard of unless you frequently read or listen to conspiracy theorists is Skull and Bones, founded at Yale University in 1832. Founders William Huntington Russell and Alphonso Taft (father of future president William Howard Taft) intentionally created a club that was elite, shrouded in secrecy, and mysterious. It was built from the start to attract rumors and conspiracy theories. Skull and Bones boasts a long list of famous and powerful people who've been members (including three generations of the Bush family: Prescott Bush, George H.W. Bush, and George W. Bush) and heads of businesses and corporations.

Conspiracy theorists believe it was membership in the secret order that helped these people rise to their lofty positions, but we can tear that one down right away. If you're from a wealthy and influential family, you're already several steps ahead in the game to become a wealthy and influential person, and if you attend Yale, your relation to a wealthy and powerful family almost guarantees you'll be invited to join the society. It's unlikely any of these people would've ended up as failures without being a member of the society.

The last secret society I'll mention is the most recent and the biggest influence in creating the idea that there's a collection of secret elite who are deciding the fate of the world. To a degree, it was formed for that purpose.

Bilderberg, named after its first meeting place—the Hotel de Bilderberg in the Netherlands—was first convened by Prince Bernhard of the Netherlands in 1954. Initially, it was a private meeting of powerful politicians from Europe and North America, with the intent of fostering warmer relations between the countries at a time when the Cold War was causing negative views of the United States and the Soviet Union. There was fear that innocent countries would be the casualties in a nuclear war between the two superpowers. Presidents, prime ministers, and every sort of head of state have been invited to these meetings, which usually host a little more than 100 guests. Initially, all the guests were politicians, but over time, people in academia, finance, and media have also been invited. Members are barred from talking about anything discussed in the meetings and journalists aren't allowed to report on anything that's said or done during the meetings. At first, this might seem suspicious, but it's not hard to imagine that to get a group like this to feel comfortable voicing their concerns or ideas, anonymity and secrecy would be necessary. All these groups are frequently mentioned when talking about the Deep State, but Bilderberg is the model of what conspiracists are talking about.

Aside from groups and secret societies, almost every multibillionaire is at one time or another thought to be behind heinous secret plans that involve either controlling people or killing off large chunks of people for population control. Because he's been so closely tied to delivering vaccines to disease-ravaged countries, Bill Gates is a frequent target of such conspiracies. Additionally, being associated with technology in general and Microsoft specifically, he's frequently rumored to be using secret advances in technology to track or control people, such as the supposed chips in vaccines we mentioned earlier.

Behind Bill Gates, second place in the "Billionaires are part of the Deep State" club is someone whose history makes him an even better target, especially among right-wing conspiracy theorists: George Soros. Soros was born in Hungary in 1930 into what he described as a "non-observant Jewish family." As a teen, he survived the Nazi occupation of Hungary. After the war, he moved to England and later the United States. He studied economics and made his fortune by managing hedge funds.

He's one of the most prolific charitable givers among billionaires based on the percentage of his wealth he's given away to different causes. His charitable foundation, the Open Society Foundations, had a net worth of $32 billion in 2021, whereas Soros himself had a net worth of just more than $8 billion. He's always been a financial supporter of progressive and liberal causes, dating back to the 1970s. His donations to dissidents in the Soviet Union are often seen as a factor that led to the breakup of the Soviet Union and the independence of former Soviet states.

He didn't become heavily involved financially in politics until 2004, when he made a significant donation to help stop the re-election of George W. Bush. In 2012, he gave substantial donations in support of the re-election of Barack Obama, and in 2015 and 2016, he donated to the presidential campaign of Hillary Clinton.

His charitable donations to social causes, including racial equality, laid the groundwork for Soros to be the target of conspiracy theories around protests and, in general, social unrest. During the Occupy Wall Street movement in 2011, rumors began to circulate that Soros was paying protesters—a claim that was repeated in 2017 when there were protests resulting from the election of Donald Trump as US president and again in 2020 during nationwide protests following the death of George Floyd.

The conspiracies that circulate around Soros are a great example of the greatest flaw of Deep State conspiracy theories: They're almost always politically biased and prone to confirmation bias, meaning people look for evidence that supports their beliefs and conveniently ignore evidence that counters those beliefs.

For example, if Soros has such incredible power to influence events and elections, George W. Bush shouldn't have won re-election in 2004 and Donald Trump wouldn't have won in 2016. The 2016 election was especially flooded with conspiracies that the Deep State had already decided Hillary Clinton would win. Why did her loss not weaken the belief in the Deep State and its power? Because, as with any strongly held belief, any evidence that it might be wrong causes believers to double down on it to try to hang on to the belief. No one wants to believe they're wrong or that they've been fooled, so anything that gives them the chance to redeem their belief will be adopted immediately. In the case of the 2016 election, the most common way conservatives clung to the omnipotent Deep State belief was to believe Donald Trump was an enemy of the Deep State working behind the scenes for the benefit of the people.

Is the concept of a group of wealthy and powerful people meeting in secret to influence global economies and politics practical and rational? Yes. If such a group could agree to meet, keep it secret, and cooperate on their plans, it would make perfect sense to do it.

What would it take to carry out? Not many people would need to know about it. With the resources available to such wealthy and powerful people, it would be possible to cover up the meeting and keep the content secret. The biggest problem is the word "cooperation." Our prototype Deep State example of Bilderberg forming—in order to smooth out problems between the nations of North America and Europe, with the goal of encouraging cooperation—might or might not have worked. Because it was secret, we'll never know what they specifically tried to achieve, but history and human nature weren't on their side. To think people will be cooperative simply because they share the trait of being wealthy and powerful is naive. In many cases, their wealth and power came from being uncooperative at best and cutthroat and bloodthirsty at worst. At what point in history have financial or political competitors ever been able to agree on anything in secret that would benefit both and be applied on a global scale? Even OPEC (Organization of the Petroleum Exporting Countries), which is the biggest driver in global oil prices, has trouble getting its member states to fully agree on anything.

In general, the Deep State concept is problematic in its ability to realistically function. But what about individual Deep State conspiracies?

Does the Deep State Decide Who'll Rule & Does Your Vote Matter?

Would a group of such power and influence want to control the leadership of a country? Of course. That part of the Deep State claim is definitely on the rational and plausible end of our spectrum. Where things get tricky is in the suspected methods.

Would they rig the voting system so they could artificially create whatever result they wanted regardless of how people voted? It's the same problem we covered about the claims of the 2020 presidential election in the United States being rigged. Think about all the different local, state, and federal eyes that watch vote counts, all the different groups and people involved in the polls, and all the checks and balances set up to verify votes. Unless everyone involved in the voting process—from top to bottom—was in on it, there'd be physically no way to do it. The first time a district performed a hand recount, the fraud would be discovered—no doubt setting off a chain reaction of recounts in other districts. Involving that many people puts the plan well on the irrational end of our scale—as close to impossible as it gets.

How could such an organization manipulate election outcomes? The easiest way for a group with such resources would be to manipulate voters through propaganda. In this scenario, it's not that your vote doesn't matter; it's that you're being manipulated to cast your vote toward certain candidates. It wouldn't require too many people because such a propaganda infrastructure already exists and is a known problem. People who don't bother to vote because they figure their vote doesn't count are probably part of the manipulation. If the Deep State can't influence your vote, then they'll convince you to not vote at all. This approach to swinging elections is well on the rational and probable end of our spectrum, but it's also flawed because a surge of popular or grassroots support for a candidate could ruin the outcome. On the flip side, you could push a candidate by artificially creating what appears to be grassroots support.

In a nutshell, yes, powerful groups could very well influence the outcome of an election, but they'd do it by influencing the decision of voters, not by tampering with physical ballots or altering voting machines.

Does the Deep State Murder Famous or Powerful People Who Are Threats to Them?

Would a group of such power and influence be able to secretly pull off murders if they wanted? Yes—without a doubt. But the greater question is, why would they? Their power and influence, especially in the media, and their access to mechanisms of propaganda would make such a measure unnecessarily risky. There's almost nothing that could be exposed that they wouldn't be able to cover up without the need to kill someone, and even if they did, the murder would need to occur before anything was exposed, not after, and you're going to avoid targeting people whose deaths will get media attention. In other words, if the Deep State has knocked off people to cover their trails, you've never heard of them, and even if you have, there appeared to be nothing suspicious about it.

There's no point here in detailing most of the celebrity deaths rumored to be the result of the Deep State. Almost everyone gets tossed into that bucket: Elvis, John Lennon, Michael Jackson, Prince—there's always someone who claims the celebrity was killed because of information they had or an undesirable social influence they were encouraging. Let's look at a couple who are frequently targets of conspiracy theories.

Was Marilyn Monroe Killed by the Kennedys?

This theory has its roots in a birthday celebration thrown for President Kennedy in May 1962 at Madison Square Garden as part of a Democratic fundraising event. Marilyn sang a modified version of the "Happy Birthday" song in a sultry—and some say suggestive—way, wearing a skintight dress that was seen as scandalous for the time but fit Marilyn's image as a sex symbol. Marilyn also attended a very exclusive private party for the president that night. The first lady, Jacqueline Kennedy, didn't attend either event, which wasn't unusual for her. She rarely attended Democratic Party fundraising events and the president's actual birthday was still a week away. Marilyn's death followed less than three months later.

It's important to note that there were no widespread conspiracy theories surrounding Marilyn's death for more than a decade. The first suggestion of a conspiracy centered around the accusation that the president's brother, Robert Kennedy, had a brief affair with Marilyn and she intended to expose it, so he had her killed. This was proposed in a pamphlet released in January 1964 (less than two months after President Kennedy's assassination) by Frank A. Capell, who was at the time a leftover of 1950s Communist fearmongering. Capell didn't like the Kennedys; he thought they were Communist sympathizers who were going to destroy the country. Although he seemed to like Marilyn, he thought she was probably surrounded by secret Communists who wanted to destroy her "American image." Coming so shortly after the death of the president, Capell's suggestion was mostly ignored until the 1970s, when it was revised by others to involve an affair with the president himself instead of his brother. Switching the target to the president brought the conspiracy theory more mainstream attention. This is a common tactic with conspiracy theories: As they spread, they'll escalate the importance of the people involved.

How does this conspiracy work within a project management approach? It doesn't. There'd be no rational reason for planning to kill the world's most famous actress over an affair with a politician. There's an infrastructure of easy denial within politics and Hollywood that could be used to dispel or diminish any such rumors. Additionally, the risk involved if the plan failed or was uncovered would be far too great compared with the benefits if the plan was successful. This one also fails as a conspiracy because of the timeline of how and when it emerged. The 1970s was a decade in which conspiracy theories became mainstream because of the Watergate scandal and the previously secret documents that were being released by the government. There was a sudden rush to speculate about what other secrets weren't being released. If the government was willing to release all these documents, there must be secret operations that are even worse that aren't being revealed. Although that's most likely true, it doesn't mean that every proposed conspiracy is true. The Marilyn Monroe conspiracy falls on the unlikely end of our spectrum.

Did the British Royal Family Orchestrate the Assassination of Princess Diana?

On August 31, 1997, Princess Diana, her companion Dodi Fayed, and their driver, Henri Paul, were killed when Paul, attempting to avoid pursuit by photographers, lost control of their vehicle while traveling at high speed and crashed in the Pont de l'Alma tunnel in Paris. According to most reports, Diana survived the crash but died shortly thereafter from her injuries.

This was easily the most globally significant celebrity death of the decade—and no doubt among the top tragic celebrity deaths of the century. For the generation who had watched the marriage of Prince Charles and Diana in 1981 and followed the later drama, including their formal separation in 1992 and divorce in 1996, it ranked with the unexpected losses of President Kennedy and John Lennon as one of the top celebrity deaths of their time. Understandably, it didn't take long for rumors to start flying that British intelligence, working on behalf of the royal family, was behind the accident and death—not a difficult leap in conspiracy logic because the royal family is often seen as either associated with secret societies or being its own secret society—a big player in the Deep State.

Before putting this on the conspiracy spectrum, we need to address why people think the royal family would want Diana dead. It seems an irrationally extreme measure and very risky, with no obvious benefit.

Within five years of their fairy-tale wedding, rumors began to circulate that there was trouble in the marriage. There was speculation that Charles and Diana were having affairs, most notably Charles with Camilla Parker Bowles and Diana with her riding instructor, James Hewitt (whose resemblance to Prince Harry spawned its own theories that he's Harry's biological father). Their public appearances together were very stiff and uncomfortable, and they began making many appearances separately. After their formal separation, Diana embarked on a media campaign to intentionally outshine Charles and she most certainly became a darling of global media through her work with various charitable organizations. Some suggested the royal family saw it as a personal attack on them, creating an increasingly negative view of the royals.

In 2003, several years after her death and long after multiple conspiracy theories had started circulating, Diana's butler, Paul Burrell, published a note he claimed had been written by Diana in 1995 (after her separation from Prince Charles but a year before their divorce). In the note, she claims Charles was plotting her death, likely through an accident with her car, so he would be free to marry Parker Bowles without going through the public humiliation of a formal divorce. Another supporting theory suggested that even after the divorce, Charles wouldn't be able to remarry as long as Diana was alive. This claim is valid in that many Anglican churches, including the Church of England, follow the tradition of "until death do you part," meaning that even if you divorce, you can't remarry as long as your former spouse is still alive.

The problem with this theory is that even with Diana gone, Charles and Parker Bowles still couldn't marry within the Church of England because Parker Bowles was also divorced and her husband was still alive. If remarrying was the plan, both spouses needed to be gone and it would be odd to go through all the trouble and risk to take out the more difficult target but not get the easy one. (Charles and Camilla eventually married in a civil ceremony in 2005, three years after the Church of England relaxed its restrictions on divorced people being allowed to remarry.)

Further fuel to the rumor of the royal family planning her murder was her two-year relationship with Hasnat Khan, a British Pakistani surgeon, and then her brief relationship with Dodi Fayed. The relationship with Khan had ended in June 1997, and shortly thereafter, Diana started spending time with Fayed. This is one of the reasons there was such intense media attention surrounding the couple. The rumors suggest the royal family wasn't happy at the prospect of Diana possibly marrying and having children with a Muslim, but it's easy to see how such rumors could easily spread in a growing Islamophobic environment. These rumors gained more traction from the belief that Diana and Fayed were about to announce their engagement and that Diana was pregnant with his child. Both these rumors were widely discredited by official autopsy reports as well as reports from those close to Diana that her recent relationship with Fayed wasn't that serious. But, of course, conspiracy theorists will always claim that official reports are cover-ups.

So with those factors in mind, let's put these conspiracies through the project management approach. Hopefully, you can imagine there are complications right from the start if you plan to assassinate arguably the most famous and beloved member of the royal family and one of the most recognizable people in the world. Our first question: Is this something you'd realistically consider? That's a hard one without knowing what kind of drama occurs behind closed doors within the royal family and British intelligence. So for the sake of argument, we'll assume they're motivated to do it.

Would it take many people to carry it out? No. Very few in fact. You'd need a few skilled people within the intelligence community who already operate in an infrastructure of high security and secrecy, but you want to make sure they're on board with the plan and aren't likely to be upset by what they're doing and potentially leak it to the public.

Here's the problem: Is the time and location in Paris the place you'd pull it off? This is where the conspiracy falls apart. If the driver, Henri Paul, was somehow in on it or, as some claim, "set up" by those carrying out the plan, it's quite a coincidence that Diana and Fayed chose the very place Paul worked and that Paul was for some reason willing to sacrifice his life to carry out the plan.

If you're a secret group working on a plan with the greatest chance of success and the least chance of exposure, this wasn't the setting you'd plan for one glaring reason: the presence of photographers. There was no way to control how many photographers there'd be and how close they might be when the plan was carried out. The death of Princess Diana would result in extensive investigations, questioning every detail of everything that happened. You'd be aware of this when formulating your plan and carefully integrate it into your plan. Such an urban setting with so many uncontrollable factors would never be proposed. Diana's charitable work took her to many places around the world where there'd be better opportunities and more advanced knowledge of her whereabouts and movements.

Even if you had people following her for an extended period prior to that fateful day, waiting for the conditions to be right to carry out the plan, the specific environment at the Ritz wouldn't be conducive to your plan. You can't predict the actions of the photographers and you can't predict other traffic that might also be on the road.

If you were going to carry out a plan that night, you'd target their destination, rumored to be Fayed's private Paris estate. This would be ideal if you wanted to get rid of Diana and deflect public suspicion and hostility to Fayed and his family. You'd have a skilled sniper awaiting their arrival. You'd take out Diana but not Fayed (fueling a potential conspiracy that the Fayed family was targeting Diana, thereby deflecting suspicion away from the royal family) in a setting that's easier to control.

In a nutshell, the idea that the royals might want Diana eliminated and had the capability to do it falls on the rational end of our spectrum and could be a rational plan within the project management approach. However, the specific setting and conditions in which the accident occurred fall more toward the irrational and unlikely end of the spectrum given the number of better options that would be available.

Was Jeffrey Epstein Murdered in Jail to Keep Him Quiet?

I end Deep State conspiracy theories with this one because it's not necessarily Deep State, but it's the most frequent bucket where you'll find this conspiracy. On August 10, 2019, Jeffrey Epstein, being held on charges of sex trafficking, was found dead in his cell. His death was ruled a suicide, but the ruling was instantly questioned by the general public and Epstein's legal team.

Who was Jeffrey Epstein and why was his death an immediate target of conspiracy theories? This guy was a hit in every category of what fuels conspiracy theories. Epstein was an American financier and socialite who came to public attention mostly after his 2008 conviction for using his private island in the US Virgin Islands for sex trafficking and entertaining a "who's who" of wealthy and powerful people, including Bill Clinton, Donald Trump, and the royal family's Prince Andrew.

Epstein purchased Little St. James island in the US Virgin Islands in 1998. He made it his primary residence and seemed to have made it his own private "fantasy island." Through financial and social connections, especially after becoming connected to publishing heiress Ghislaine Maxwell, he had a long list of wealthy and powerful people who had met him, spent time with him, or accepted favors from him, such as transporting them on his private 727 and hosting them at his private island.

The first legal complaints associated with sex trafficking came in 2005. In 2008, despite more than 36 women identified as Epstein's victims, some as young as 14, he was convicted on only two counts as part of a controversial plea deal. He served only 13 months, with quite a bit of free time because of a "work release" deal, working for a company he formed himself specifically for the opportunity. Upon his release, he dissolved the company. Between 2005 and 2009, many of his high-profile acquaintances openly distanced themselves from him, but his conviction and jail sentence didn't stop his behavior. In July 2019, he was arrested again—on sex trafficking charges in Florida and New York—and this time, evidence was collected from his New York residence.

It had been claimed by people who'd worked for Epstein at his residences—in New York and on the private island—that he had secret video cameras everywhere and a stash of incriminating videos of his various guests as "insurance" against any claims against him or if he needed favors. These videos were rumored to be why he received a generous plea deal and easy "jail" time in 2005 despite the charges and number of victims. When his New York residence was searched during his arrest in 2019, these rumors were confirmed with the discovery of pin cameras, photo albums, hard drives, and CDs containing photos and videos.

You can see why so many conspiracy theories would immediately spring up when Epstein died in custody and alone in his cell. There's an additional fly in the ointment: Three weeks prior to his death, he was found unconscious in his cell with wounds to his neck. He shared the cell with former police officer Nicholas Tartaglione, who was being held on four counts of murder. The cellmate was later cleared of any involvement, but it was never exactly clear what had happened. It was declared a suicide attempt, and Epstein was briefly isolated and placed on suicide watch.

He was later moved to a secure housing unit, where he was assigned a cellmate and guards were to check on him every 30 minutes. On the evening of August 9th, the cellmate was transferred, the guards assigned to him supposedly fell asleep and failed to check on him, and the security cameras that should have been watching his cell failed to work.

At 6:30 a.m. on the morning of August 10th, he was found dead in his cell. He was removed from the cell as attempts were supposedly made to resuscitate him. This meant the original scene was disturbed and there were no pictures taken of Epstein's position or condition when he was found.

It's not hard to see why so many consider the death suspicious and you can probably see why I said his death is a hit on almost every factor that can fuel a conspiracy theory. Too many coincidental things were being done wrong or going wrong preceding his death.

A secret life with a private island, sex trafficking charges, associations with an enormous number of wealthy and powerful people over a period of decades—how could this not result in multiple conspiracy theories?

There are several different conspiracies that float around:

- He killed himself because he knew his time was up and he didn't want the evidence found at his residence to be revealed in court.
- A person or group wanted him dead for the same reason—to prevent any discovered evidence from being revealed in court.
- A person or group orchestrated the arrest in the first place with the goal of getting access to Epstein's residence and taking possession of the photos and videos and then eliminated him before he could give a statement or be put on trial.
- Epstein didn't actually die; it was all staged so he could escape.

I'll address these individually because there are a few variations within them and some are more valid than others.

Theory #1: Epstein Killed Himself

We'll start with the official story. Is this a valid possibility? Given the likely charges against him and the evidence found at his residence, he'd be facing a humiliating trial and a long prison sentence. The presence of the video evidence would make it unlikely he could swing another easy plea bargain.

But there's a variation to this: Remember that he'd been on suicide watch several weeks earlier because of what seemed like a suicide attempt? Some believe he did this to be moved to an isolated unit where he didn't have to share a cell with another prisoner. Could he have been trying this again and died accidentally because no one found him in time? He believed there were live cameras watching him and guards who'd check on him every 30 minutes. He expected to be found quickly and moved to another cell. Instead, no one was watching and he wasn't found until long after he was dead.

What about the incredible coincidence that his cellmate had just been moved, the cameras were off, and the guards didn't check on him for hours? Is there a rational explanation for all those factors coming together at just the right time? Yes. We're assuming that the cameras being off and the guards being asleep was an unusual event that never happened. Realistically, video is insurance if something out of the ordinary happens so it can be reviewed. It's unlikely anyone ever checks entire videos from uneventful evenings.

It's possible that because Epstein's cellmate had just been moved and Epstein was alone, the only task the guards had was to check on him every half hour, and considering that Epstein was likely going to sleep through it, why not just shut off the camera (so if someone did check later, there's no evidence they weren't monitoring the cell) and kick back to take a nap for a couple hours? This could be something the guards had done in the past without getting caught, so they did it again, but this time, something happened. So it's not three events happening coincidentally at the same time (prisoner moved, cameras off, guards asleep); it's one event leading to the other two. If you've ever worked a graveyard shift where nothing happens, this scenario doesn't sound unrealistic at all.

Before we move on, there's another "accidental death" possibility that might explain the attempt weeks earlier and the final attempt that resulted in his death: autoerotic asphyxiation, in which during an orgasm, oxygen is cut off to the brain (by a partner's hands or something wrapped around the neck and tightened), causing an increased intensity to the orgasm. It's suggested to never do this alone because of the risk of passing out before restoring normal blood flow to the brain, but if you're a sex trafficker sitting in a jail cell, what else is there to do?

There's one more possibility that makes a good transition between suicide and murder: He killed himself because he was told if he didn't do it, someone would do it for him and it would be much less pleasant. All the coincidental factors were manufactured to give him the opportunity.

All these theories fall on the rational and possible end of our conspiracy spectrum given who Epstein was, who he knew, what he'd done, the evidence against him, and what he was facing. This leads us to the next theory.

Theory #2: Epstein Was Murdered

First off, would killing Epstein in jail after his arrest be a rational plan someone might realistically attempt with an expectation of success? Keep in mind, as opposed to many of the other conspiracy theories in this book, we have confirmed evidence that wealthy and famous people visited Epstein's residences either on the mainland or the island,

and there's video and photo evidence of their behavior during these visits. If this behavior could be career-ending or illegal, it would create tremendous motivation to use whatever resources and influence are available to reduce risk and get rid of evidence. So yes, there'd be rational motivation for someone with the resources and influence at high levels to make the attempt to kill Epstein.

We're going to primarily focus on the likelihood of rich and powerful people having Epstein killed to keep him from talking, but there's another possibility we need to address first. Most of the murder scenarios assume the guards were involved in some way: either getting out of the way so the killers could get to Epstein or being paid or instructed to kill him themselves. However, it's also possible that one or both guards killed him without any outside influence or instruction simply because of who he was and what he'd done, and they tried to make it look like a suicide. Would that count as rational and possible? Yes. The means and motivation are there as well as a reasonable belief they could get away with it. It also could have been accidental. They roughed him up, it got out of hand, and he died, so they staged it to look like a suicide. This would also explain the different interpretations of the autopsy results as looking like hanging and strangulation. We'll cover the autopsy issue in a moment.

Why did someone want him dead this time and not the first time he was arrested? Wouldn't there be equal motivation both times? What happened between the first arrest, conviction, and jail time that made it worth getting rid of him this time? There could be any number of personal reasons one of his acquaintances would jump to such an extreme upon the second arrest when they didn't after the first arrest, but the most likely is something I mentioned earlier: photo and video evidence. There was no such evidence the first time, so even if Epstein could be trusted to remain silent, killing him was the only way to keep the evidence from being exposed in court. (In spite of this, some evidence was submitted during the trial of Ghislaine Maxwell in 2021.)

Given the time of day when Epstein died, the number of people who had access to him during that time, and the ability to disable the cameras near his cell, it wouldn't take very many people to carry it out. Equally, the supposed suicide attempt weeks earlier creates immediate support for the idea that he tried again and was successful this time.

What about another version of this conspiracy?

Theory #3: Epstein's Arrest & Murder Were All Planned in Advance in Order To Take Possession of the Evidence & Get Epstein Out of the Way

In spite of how it sounds, this one also falls on the rational and possible side of our spectrum. It fits the project management approach as a plan someone could be expected to attempt and would require very few people to be in on because most of the people carrying it out would be following legitimate law enforcement procedures. All that's needed is a few influential people at the top of the authority chain to start the ball rolling.

According to this conspiracy, most of Epstein's guests were unaware that he was recording their activities as "insurance" until his first arrest. At that time, he used some of that insurance to motivate people in high places to put pressure on prosecutors, leading to a very generous plea deal and relatively easy "jail" time. This caused his high-profile guests to realize he was a threat to them. It was after the first arrest that many of his associates openly distanced themselves from him. Imagine yourself as one of his past guests. You engaged in some behavior at the private island that would be damaging to you if it ever became public and you've learned he has video of what you did. Wouldn't you be motivated to find those videos and destroy them? Or at least get them away from Epstein? Of course you would.

There were more than 30 victims associated with Epstein's first arrest, but the plea deal resulted in only two charges. That's a big resource to pull new evidence, drop the evidence into the right hands, drop tips about what kind of evidence could be found and where it could be found, and then let the police do their work. If you have high-level influence, especially political influence, it would be very easy to pull this off. The police then arrest Epstein and seize the evidence. If Epstein ends up dead, the evidence might end up sealed or at least stored in a place where you could access and destroy it. Mission accomplished. Rational and possible.

Again, I'm not personally endorsing any of these or suggesting they happened, but the influence and corruption infrastructure is already there if someone were motivated to pull the strings.

What about the final bullet point? Epstein either by himself or with the assistance of associates staged his death so he could disappear. There are different versions of this one, so I'll address them individually.

Theory #4a: Epstein Planned a Staged Suicide After His Arrest to Escape Authorities

Supporters of this one claim Epstein's first suicide attempt was to plant the idea he might kill himself and cause him to be moved to a different cell, where the plan could be carried out more easily. There are three versions of how he escaped. First, he escaped while the guards were out and the cameras were off and a body similar to his was placed in his cell, so he was long gone by the time it was found.

Second, he was faking being dead and the guards, who were in on it, removed him from the cell and switched him with another body before putting it in the ambulance. Lastly, he was faking his death while being removed from the prison and put in the ambulance, and he was switched en route (ambulance driver was in on it) or at the hospital.

Would these be a plan someone might design and try to carry out if they had the resources to influence people to participate? Given what Epstein was facing and the influence he had with people in high positions, yes. It wouldn't take very many people. The guards most likely need to be in on it and possibly the ambulance driver, but New York City's chief medical examiner, Barbara Sampson, who performed the autopsy, and the independent pathologist, Michael Baden, hired by Epstein's lawyers, would also need to take part.

The problem with this? If those people were in on it, there would've been nothing in their results to cause questions about the cause of death and Epstein's lawyers would've never questioned the results and suggested it wasn't suicide. Questions were raised about broken bones found in the neck being inconsistent with suicide and more commonly associated with strangulation, and Epstein's choice of strangling himself with part of a bedsheet was odd when there were better materials available in his cell. (Also raising the question: Why would there be such materials in the cell of someone who had recently been on suicide watch?)

If Epstein had hidden his plans from his lawyers so they'd think he was really dead and the chief medical examiner wasn't in on it, such reactions would make sense—with one major flaw: They'd know the body they were given to autopsy wasn't Epstein's. Overall, the faking of a body or replacement with another dead body is problematic and makes this theory very unlikely. Someone else must be dead. They have to at least look like Epstein. The body needs to be snuck into or near the jail and it needs to fool a forensic autopsy. Unless, of course, the people performing the autopsy are in on it, and as I mentioned, if they were in on it, the autopsy would've been very clean with no suspicious findings to draw attention. Overall, this version of the conspiracy fails the project management approach and falls on the unlikely end of our spectrum, which leads to one that's a little more sound.

Theory #4b: Epstein's Arrest and Faked Suicide Were Part of a Plea Deal with Authorities

In this one, the authorities are not only in on it, but it's also their plan. What's the goal? To get access to Epstein's library of photos and videos to build cases against high-profile pedophiles, perhaps with interest in one or two specific cases. The fake suicide prevents Epstein from facing any charges at all and protects him from enemies who might seek revenge for him turning over the evidence.

Is this a plan someone might realistically plan and intend to carry out with an expectation of success? If they had the available resources and potential for security, yes. In this variation of the plan, key authorities, including the chief medical examiner, were in on it. The suspicious autopsy results create the same problem as in the previous conspiracy unless we tweak one important aspect. In this scenario, no one in Epstein's inner circle, including his lawyers, were in on it. They'd believe he was dead. Therefore, the unexpected independent pathologist who was present at the autopsy was the problem. The medical examiner couldn't fully fake the findings when another expert was there observing. They had to present a recent death who looked similar enough to fool someone who wasn't personally acquainted with Epstein and who died by a method similar to hanging. In this case, the substitute body died from strangulation. It's close enough for someone to tweak the results to fit hanging but not close enough to fool an independent pathologist. This would make Epstein's lawyers suspicious and claim it was murder instead of suicide.

Would law enforcement officials attempt something like this? It sounds more like the plot of a movie or TV drama than anything the legal system would attempt. But yes, given the high stakes of getting evidence on powerful and wealthy people who might be connected to sex trafficking and people with resources to cover their tracks and pay the best lawyers, having indisputable photo or video evidence would be a temptation that might make the risk worth it. As far-fetched as it might seem, this one leans toward the rational and probable end of our spectrum. When you think about it, it's not much different from helping a mob informant disappear through a witness relocation program.

Before we leave Epstein, I know there's one burning question you want me to answer: If Epstein were murdered, who was most likely behind it? You want me to say Donald Trump, Bill Clinton, or Prince Andrew because those are the three most high-profile and publicly important people associated over the years with Epstein. Unfortunately, Epstein had hundreds, probably thousands, of guests at his residences—many of whom hold positions of political and economic importance. Many of them are people you might have never heard of because they don't attract the mass media or pop culture attention. If Epstein were murdered, the culprit was most likely someone or a collection of people who are very important, are very powerful, and would have a lot to lose from either the public humiliation or legal liability of their actions at one or more of Epstein's private "parties" being leaked to the public. Of the three I mentioned, you're no doubt most suspicious and most certain of the guilt of whomever you dislike the most for politically biased reasons.

Sorry, but everyone who's ever traveled and socialized with Epstein is forever equally on the suspect list.

That brings us to a related conspiracy.

The "Clinton Body Count" or the "Hillary Hit List"

The original "Hillary Hit List" referred to a list of people Hillary Clinton felt betrayed her during the 2008 Democratic primaries when she started strong but eventually lost the nomination to Barack Obama. It later evolved on propaganda websites into a supposed list of people Hillary had killed because they had some dirt on her that could be damaging. The original "Clinton Body Count" dates back to the Clintons' time in Arkansas and refers to rumors that Bill and Hillary Clinton had enemies killed in order to keep sensitive or damaging information from being exposed.

There's a big glaring problem with these rumors. If the Clintons can so easily and so secretly get rid of people who are problems, why have so many people come forward and caused the Clintons problems? Why are so many people on the "hit list" either random acquaintances whose "damaging information" is simply speculated or people who've already been problems and can do no further damage?

If the Clintons had the power and influence to pull off such a string of assassinations without ever being discovered, they could have easily prevented all the scandals that tainted their image. They'd appear to be the cleanest, most honest, and scandal-free political couple in the country. Hillary would've easily won the nomination in 2008 or at the very least would've easily won the presidential election in 2016.

It's not hard to see the propaganda tactics used in these accusations. If a person dies of any official cause and they can be linked to ever having any kind of connection to the

Clintons or even more broadly to the Democratic National Committee, it's seen as another Clinton "hit." If a scandal is being investigated in a foreign country and a key witness is killed, there will be claims the Clintons were being investigated and they killed the witness. It's even easier if the Clinton charitable foundation has ever been involved in that country. The people who want most to believe in this conspiracy will almost never fact-check the claims.

This one fails our test for one very big reason: the number and variety of investigations over the years carried out by Clinton opponents without uncovering any evidence of homicidal activity. Again, if they were that powerful and had the resources to create such clean cover-ups without leaving any evidence, Hillary would've served two terms as president already.

How Would a Deep State Organization Work?

Let's run the idea of a powerful and secret Deep State through the project management approach. Would it be rational and viable, and how would you organize it and run it? We need to start by anchoring a key point: A real Deep State group wouldn't operate with the same pure evil and malice usually represented in movies, TV, and conspiracy theories. They'd be very smart and manipulate the rules in a way that would allow them to operate well within the rules and they'd be very risk-averse with their plans.

Not only would it be rational and viable to attempt, but if we're to consider the most likely origin, it would be a group that formed completely by accident—simply through wealthy and powerful people meeting on occasion and brainstorming ways to manipulate the general public in the best interests of the wealthy and powerful. This wouldn't be a recent creation. It would've most likely started around the time of the

Industrial Revolution, when the expansion of industry created mega-wealth and mega-influence and the population of cities began to explode as more people moved away from rural areas and into cities to work in factories. Over time, these "influence" groups might bring in others who have a vested interest or are able to help the group achieve their goals. At first, you'd have mostly businesspeople, but along the way, you'd pick up some politicians.

Why not politicians right from the start? Because their careers can be short, and after leaving office, they have little value to your group. Their knowledge that your group exists would be a loose end. If politicians are being brought into your group, it will be people who had power and influence before entering politics and whose power and influence will likely continue after leaving office.

We can even blend in a couple earlier conspiracy theories in a logical way. Would you seek out people who've been members of secret societies? Yes, that would be rational and likely. Why? Because to become a member of such a society, you probably already come from wealth and power. Being a member of such a group demonstrates your ability to operate within a secret group and effectively protect its secrecy. For example, George H.W. Bush was a member of Skull and Bones, and long before he was vice president and president, he was director of the CIA. That's an attractive résumé for being brought into a Deep State group. Even after losing his presidential re-election campaign, he likely maintained great influence compared with other politicians whose political careers had ended.

How would the Deep State get control of politicians without bringing them directly into the group or making them aware of the group? According to movies and TV, you'd be very heavy-handed and threatening. "Here's what we want. You're going to do it or we're going to cap you off and everyone important to you." Not only would there be no need for that, but it would create unnecessary loose ends and vendettas. There's a much easier way.

Here's a completely hypothetical example. We're in the Deep State organization and we're trying to expand our technological influence around the world, but the United States has some tech regulations in place that prevent us from achieving these goals. Under the guise of a typical political action group, we approach a variety of candidates running for office and tell them we have millions of dollars we can put into their campaigns. All we want in return is their promise that they'll support legislation to change these regulations. If they ask why we want them changed, we simply point out that the change will expand our business opportunities and therefore not just benefit us but also the national economy overall.

We do this across multiple candidates for the House and Senate in different states. If they agree, we pour our money and influence into their campaigns to help them get elected. It might take several election cycles before we have enough people in place, but our plans are generally long term. As for those candidates who didn't agree, are they loose ends who might reveal the manipulative tactics of the Deep State? No. They have no idea we're Deep State. They think we were a typical wealthy group trying to get politicians elected who can help our businesses.

Let me stop for a moment and point out a difference between the reality of a Deep State group, which is on the rational and likely end of our spectrum, versus the typical Deep State represented in conspiracy theories and fiction. The conspiracy and fiction versions operate in a stereotypical evil way that's not logical or rational and would have no long-term practical application. Those versions are farther down our spectrum toward the irrational end. They'd involve too many people and create too many dangerous loose ends and the assumption they kill their enemies would introduce a degree of risk that would create paranoia and fear within the group, quickly causing it to fragment and dissolve.

In the modern era of social media, the mass media, and everyone carrying cell phones with cameras, how could a Deep State group meet without leaving clues that multiple powerful people were all showing up in the same place around the same time? If you were in such a group, would you trust technology enough to have secret meetings virtually? There's an easy solution to those issues that would allow communication while maintaining secrecy. Each member of the group would have a trusted associate who's not known to the general public and who'd be briefed on the goals and then sent to the meeting.

Much like the Illuminati, each member would be identified by a nickname known only to the other members of the group. Each associate would identify by the nickname of the person they're representing. None of the associates would know who's identified by the nicknames other than the one they're representing. So if anyone were to go rogue, they couldn't expose anyone other than the person they're representing. The meeting would be recorded and copied to flash drives for the associate to return to the member.

Even if the associate were to copy the recording and release it to the public, it says nothing about who was being represented and there's no proof the associate ever gave a flash drive to the member. The rogue associate could easily be branded as a disgruntled employee and "conspiracy nut" trying to create trouble or even attempting blackmail. When the members did want to directly communicate, it would be through coded messages. Notifications of meeting times and locations would be delivered through traditional "snail mail" hard-copy messages.

Obviously, this form of such a group wouldn't be as exciting as what's represented in fictional media and in conspiracy theories, but as I said, this is the version that would be on the rational and possible end of our spectrum.

Before we leave this section, let me give you one last mind-bender: Everything you think you know about the Deep State—all the rumors and leaks and pieces of information carefully connected by conspiracy theorists—was all created by the Deep State itself. Much like the military creating and perpetuating UFO conspiracies in order to cover up secret aircraft, the Deep State would be the biggest manufacturer of Deep State rumors and conspiracies. More generally, any extreme conspiracy theory. The more extreme, the better. Why? To create the stereotype of conspiracy theorists being tinfoil hat–wearing nutjobs, so the very existence of a Deep State itself is more likely to be labeled a crackpot conspiracy theory.

We have one last category to cover in Chapter 12: Let's bring down the temperature a bit and dive into some pop culture conspiracy theories.

CHAPTER 12

POP CULTURE CONSPIRACY THEORIES

We've covered some very dark topics in this book: political assassinations, celebrity murders, the intentional killing of millions of people for population control, powerful elites secretly planning to control the world, etc. We'll end it with something lighter. Pop culture conspiracies have little consequence for the general public and they're usually simply "conspiracies of deception" that serve supporting roles in leaning people toward belief that secret things happen; therefore, the bigger conspiracies might be true. These run the gamut of celebrities faking their deaths or dying and being replaced to simple conspiracies of deceptive marketing. These are the fluff of the conspiracy world, but we'll apply the same criteria to these that we applied to all the others.

Famous People Who Died & Were Replaced by Look-Alikes

The claim: Beatle Paul McCartney was killed in a car accident in 1966 and replaced with a look-alike named Billy Shears. The band never publicly admitted the death and switch but put clues on all their following albums. The name of the replacement is mentioned at the end of the opening song on the *Sgt. Pepper's Lonely Hearts Club Band* album.

The back cover, which for the first time included printed lyrics to all the songs, has George Harrison pointing to the line "Wednesday morning at 5 o'clock," the time of the accident. The song "A Day in the Life" describes the accident. The line "Nobody was really sure if he was from the House of Lords" suggests a member of the government but is actually the line "Nobody was really sure if he was from the House or Paul," meaning someone from the House of Parliament or Paul McCartney.

On the US release of *Magical Mystery Tour*, there's a photo montage from the TV movie included in the fold-out album. One of the pictures is McCartney sitting at a desk with a nameplate in front of him that says "I was." In the final dance scene in the movie, McCartney is the only one wearing a black flower on his suit.

On the *White Album*, the song "Glass Onion" includes John Lennon singing the line "Well here's another clue for you all: The Walrus was Paul," referring to the song "I Am the Walrus," which some conspiracy supporters believe is a representation of death or a corpse. Also on the *White Album*, after Lennon's song "I'm So Tired," Lennon seems to mumble something in French before the next song. If you play it backward, it sounds like "Paul is dead, man. Miss him. Miss him." And in the song "Revolution 9," if you play the repeating line "Number 9, number 9, number 9" backward, it sounds like "Turn me on, dead man."

On the front cover of *Abbey Road*, the Beatles are shown crossing the street. Conspiracy believers claim it shows the Beatles leaving a graveyard: Lennon is dressed as a priest, Ringo Starr as an undertaker, Harrison as a gravedigger, and McCartney is the corpse because he's the only one barefoot. Another clue that this is Billy Shears, not Paul McCartney, is that "Paul" is holding his cigarette in his right hand, but the real McCartney was left-handed. In the background is a VW *Beetle* with the license plate "28IF," meaning Paul would've been 28 if he'd lived. On the back cover of the album, there's a crack running through the "S" in Beatles, indicating a disruption in the group.

The conspiracy is thought to have started with a call to a Detroit radio station in October 1969, but it has its roots back in 1967, when the *Sgt. Pepper's Lonely Hearts Club Band* album was first released. It gained traction with the release of each subsequent Beatles album and the supposed additional clues. Public appearances and denials by Paul McCartney himself claiming to be alive and be the real person didn't diminish the growth of the conspiracy and there are some today who still believe it.

Before applying our criteria to this conspiracy, let's talk about why a conspiracy like this would form in the first place. The most likely root is the world of literature, where it's not uncommon for a ghostwriter to write books credited to someone else or even to take up the name of a successful writer after their death and continue publishing books under their name. Author V.C. Andrews, famous for the novel *Flowers in the Attic*, has published more than 50 books, but the majority were ghostwritten by writer Andrew Neiderman after her death under contract with her estate. Andrews herself only wrote seven of the books attributed to her name. Ever notice those rows of James Patterson novels on the bookshelf? He seems like one of the most prolific authors in history, but he's known to simply write notes and outlines and then have ghostwriters complete the books.

So how does the "Paul is dead" conspiracy fit into a project management approach? What would it take to cover up the death of a Beatle and replace him with a look-alike? There are two parts to this: You need to cover up the initial death of one of the most famous people in the world without it leaking to the public at all and you also have to make the replacement disappear from his regular life to take on the new role. The new McCartney can't just look like him; he also must sound like him and play the same instruments with the same skill.

It's argued that "Billy Shears" took time to learn to play an instrument, which is why the Beatles stopped touring. But what happened to Billy Shears, who supposedly looked so much like the real McCartney that he could replace him? Did he fake his own death? Did his family and friends report him missing? It would take a lot of people to keep this one quiet, and given the amount of effort it would take, why would you put clues on your albums revealing it?

There's a counterconspiracy theory to this one, which has all the same problems but is stronger in one area. The counter theory is that John Lennon was the one who died in an accident and was replaced. His replacement sounded almost exactly like him but didn't look exactly like him, so they changed his hairstyle and had him start wearing glasses. Looking at the Beatles in 1966 versus 1967, Lennon is the one whose appearance seems to change the most. But again, it has all the same problems: keeping it a secret and all the people it would take. Also, why leave clues on the albums?

The bigger project management question is this: Why are they doing this? The plan would have had to go into action immediately, silencing people at the scene of the accident who recognize the famous victim and people at the hospital where the body is taken—and you hope there are no initial reports or rumors before you can silence them. And what's the benefit? Is the band going to fade away to obscurity because of the loss of one member? There was no precedent for that at the time. Later, the Rolling Stones lost Brian Jones but replaced him and continued. The Who lost Keith Moon but continued. It makes no practical sense to cover up the death and replace the member with someone who looks and sounds like him, continue as if nothing happened, then plant clues on future albums.

You might have already thought of a problem with the *Abbey Road* cover and McCartney holding a cigarette in his right hand. If he was a right-handed replacement, he did a very good job in the famous rooftop concert and all later public appearances with Wings and as a solo artist in playing his bass left-handed. If you look at pictures of the Beatles earlier in their career, before McCartney's supposed death, you can see he often held his cigarette in his right hand, especially when using his left hand for another task.

All these "killed and replaced" conspiracies fall on the unlikely and irrational side of the spectrum because of the number of people they'd take and how difficult it would be to cover up the initial death. Think of how quickly the media reported the death of John Lennon in 1980 or Princess Diana in 1997. There'd be no time to put a cover-up in place before word got out. Looking back at media reports in 1966, there were no reports at all of an accident in which the victim was initially reported as Paul McCartney and then later changed to someone else (such as Billy Shears, which would be a convenient way to get rid of his original identity).

A more recent "dead and replaced" conspiracy involves singer Avril Lavigne, who by official account is very much alive but supposedly died in 2003 shortly after the release of her first album and was replaced by a look-alike named Melissa Vandella, who'd been hired as a body double for public appearances. After Lavigne's death, Vandella was given singing lessons in order to continue Lavigne's career for the record label. This rumor started on a Brazilian blog in 2011 and is based on changes in Avril's physical appearance between 2003 and 2011 (normal changes with age and with changes in makeup style) and the supposed disappearance of birthmarks and blemishes.

This one is more on the rational side of our conspiracy spectrum because it involves a solo artist rather than a member of a group and Lavigne's fame was still young enough that she might not be recognized as the victim of an unexpected death. This also parallels the examples we started with of author estates hiring ghostwriters to continue the career of a famous name after they died. There's still the problem of the number of people who'd know about the cover-up, such as Lavigne's family and friends, as well as the family and friends of the replacement.

But much like the fictional Hannah Montana, it wouldn't be out of the question for the double to continue living her normal life as someone who happens to look a lot like Avril Lavigne and only assume the Lavigne role when needed for public appearances. Recording sessions wouldn't be a problem because no one there needs to know the person singing isn't the original Lavigne, and much like author V.C. Andrews, by this point, most of the Avril Lavigne discography has been a product of the double. I'm not saying this one is true—I lean on the side of believing Avril is the original Avril—but even from a project management approach, it's something that might be viable from a record industry standpoint.

And since I mentioned Hannah Montana, Miley Cyrus was also subject of a "died and was replaced by a double" rumor near the end of her Hannah Montana years. This one received a boost during the 2007–2008 Hannah/Miley tour, when Miley played both characters. Her publicist admitted they did use a double to finish one of the songs while Miley went backstage for costume changes. This one falls on the spectrum around the same spot as the Avril Lavigne theories for the same reasons.

Replacement theories that fall on the irrational end of the spectrum involve anything claiming a celebrity has been replaced by biologically manufactured clones because, of course, the technology isn't there to be producing a bunch of rapidly aged adult duplicates through cloning. Such celebrities rumored to be replaced—sometimes multiple times—by clones include Megan Fox, Britney Spears, and Taylor Swift. To delve a little more into the bizarre, there are claims that Katy Perry is actually a grown-up JonBenét Ramsey, which would mean Ramsey wasn't really murdered, which would raise the questions: Whose body was found? Why fake her death? And after going through all that trouble, why raise her to be a public figure with a completely falsified history? We won't even bother with the project management teardown of that one because the magnitude of such a cover-up and re-emergence as a new person would be completely impractical and unnecessary.

Celebrities Who Faked Their Deaths to Live Normal, Anonymous Lives

Almost every famous person, especially those beloved by fans, has been the subject of this one, famously starting with Elvis Presley. As of 2022, Elvis would be more than 85 years old, but there are still people who claim to have spotted him. Steve Jobs has supposedly been spotted in different countries around the world since his death, as have John Lennon, Michael Jackson, Tupac Shakur, and the Notorious B.I.G., to name a few.

What fuels these? True cases of individuals who've purposely faked their deaths and adopted new identities, usually nonfamous people who are trying to escape unhappy marriages, avoid criminal charges, or escape financial debt. So because this is something that happens, doesn't it make sense that rich and famous people would also have the resources to do this?

Yes. But they also have the resources and options to disappear without the need to fake their deaths. Celebrities fall off the radar all the time. John Lennon himself did it in the years before his death when he stopped recording and stopped making public appearances. He talked about being able to take walks around New York and rarely be bothered as long as he stayed out of the media. There are numerous flaws with the idea that celebrities would fake their deaths in the hopes of suddenly becoming anonymous:

- It makes no sense to go out in public undisguised and risk being spotted; most of the claims of celebrities faking their deaths come from people who claim to see the people out in public.
- You can disguise yourself when you go out in public and usually not be recognized, even without faking your death.
- You'd either give up your monetary resources and be poor or you must fake your last will and testament and inevitably leave a paper trail when transferring assets to your new identity.
- You're not only giving up your identity, but you're also giving up the profession that made you famous. To continue the profession under a new identity would risk becoming famous again or being recognized.

In a nutshell, a new identity would have more downside and added risks than simply leaving your profession and stepping out of the spotlight.

New Coke Was a Cover to Hide the Formula Change in Classic Coke

Although Coke was the number one soft drink beverage in 1985 (by sales), it had been gradually losing market share to other beverages and blind taste tests confirmed most people seemed to prefer the sweeter taste of Pepsi. In response, Coke introduced a new formula with a sweeter taste and the result was a disaster. Coke drinkers hated it. Three months later, the original formula returned and was rebranded as "Classic Coke," while the new formula retained the "Coke" label. Sales of Classic Coke skyrocketed beyond the sales prior to the introduction of the new formula. In 1990, the "Classic" formula reclaimed the singular Coke label and the new formula became "Coke II." The new formula was finally discontinued in 2002.

This is typically seen as a cautionary tale of the danger of tampering with a proven formula, but conspiracy theorists believe the disaster of the new formula was intentional. Their argument is that original Coke was briefly taken off the market in favor of a different-tasting formula so the company could change the ingredients of the original formula without people noticing. They claim when Classic Coke returned, it wasn't the same as original Coke.

This conspiracy theory falls well on the rational and likely side of the spectrum because they're right about one thing: There was something different about Classic Coke that might have been noticed if not for the three-month absence of the original formula. Original Coke was made with sugar, but Classic Coke shifted to high-fructose corn syrup—a subtle change that the average drinker might not notice, but Coke purists would've noticed it if given a side by side comparison. This has been demonstrated by comparisons between Coke bottled in Mexico (which uses pure cane sugar) versus Coke bottled in the United States (using high-fructose corn syrup).

Would it make sense to risk your market share by taking a sales hit with the new formula? From a project management perspective, this does make sense because if drinkers notice the difference between sugar and corn syrup, you might permanently lose market, but if there's a three-month hiatus where they're given a drastically new formula compared with the old formula, then when it returns, you have a better shot at retaining (and maybe increasing) sales and market share.

Again, I don't say this one is true, but of all the conspiracy theories we've covered in this book, this is the one I'd be least surprised if it turned out to be true.

The National Football League Is Scripted

The general idea here is that much like pro wrestling, the NFL determines which team is going to win before the game is ever played and designs wins and losses for maximum market appeal. Every season, you'll see this theory supported and spread on any given week by fans who feel their team's loss was because of being "cheated" by the referees.

Would the league be motivated to control the outcome of games for maximum market profit? Of course.

Would it take very many people to carry it out and keep it secret? That depends on the specifics of the theory. If you believe the players themselves are aware of the scripted outcome and play to produce the scripted result, then there are too many people involved to keep it secret and too many random factors that have to be controlled, such as the ability of a receiver to make or miss a catch based on the script or a kicker to make or miss a field goal or extra point. Such an environment would've been exposed long ago by a disgruntled player being forced out of the league.

On the other hand, the referees can influence the outcome of a game based on the penalties they call. That's a much smaller group to manage and not all the referees need to be in on it. You only need one or two in any given game to help influence the outcome. For example, in today's NFL, a referee could potentially call a holding penalty on any play. So a rigged NFL using a handful of referees to produce a desired outcome is on the rational and possible end of our spectrum.

However, I'd suggest there's evidence the league isn't rigged. If so, they'd always end up with the most marketable—or at least one of the top most marketable—matchups for the Super Bowl because they want teams with the broadest national appeal. But they often end up with poorly marketable teams and relatively boring games.

The Government Is Monitoring All Your Phone Calls or Listening to You Through Electronic Devices in Your Home

All your phone calls are being monitored and your voice assistants are always listening and recording what you're saying and doing. Even your microwave and coffee pot probably have monitoring chips in them sending information to the government.

Is it rational or viable that this is happening? No, at least insofar as the entire population is being monitored. Imagine the technological infrastructure required to maintain all that data and how many people would be required to listen. Even if computers handled the listening and tagged certain content for a human to review, you'd still be talking about millions of pieces of data every day. They'd be one of the largest employers in the world, and again, no one is stepping forward to expose it. Wouldn't that have been part of the information Edward Snowden revealed?

And not to insult people, but why do you think you're so important that the government would want to listen to you in your home or track your movements?

You know who'd be interested? Private, profit-driven companies who have products to sell. They might want to listen for keywords in order to suggest specific products to you, but there's nothing of value the government is going to get by listening to you.

Is it viable that private companies would monitor you in such a way? Could they use computers to listen for keywords and associate those words with products they can suggest? Not really. Right now, the algorithms that would be listening to you wouldn't be able to understand the context, so any word that happens to be the name of a product might end up becoming a suggestion. Currently, companies use purchase history and cookies that they and other sites leave on your computer to decipher what you might or might not like, and at the moment, that's much more accurate than listening to you all the time and grabbing keywords.

In a nutshell, if you carry a cell phone, you can be tracked. If you purchase items online, your credit or debit card information is potentially out there and your purchase history can be tracked. No one needs to be listening to you. You're freely handing them all the information they'd need to profile you.

Birds Are All Dead—They've Been Replaced by Government Spy Drones & They Recharge by Sitting on Power Lines

I end on a light note with this one because it was started as a joke making fun of conspiracy theorists, even though I wouldn't be surprised if there were people somewhere who truly believe it or at least believe that *some* birds are secretly government spy drones.

Just for fun, let's put this on our spectrum. It's way on the irrational side and fails the project management test simply by pure volume of drones, the number of people who'd have to be aware of it, the manufacturing infrastructure to build them would be one of the largest manufacturers in the world and employ tens of thousands of people, and the technological infrastructure to control them and store the data would be immense. From manufacturing to operation to data collection and storage, you'd easily employ 100,000 people and not even one of those people ever went public with the information. It has the same infrastructure problem as the idea of the government monitoring everyone.

I must admit, though, the idea that bird drones charge by sitting on power lines is pretty clever.

There are many more we could cover, but by now, you have an idea of the criteria we'd apply to them and how rational/likely or irrational/unlikely they'd be. And that was pretty much the point of the book.

Afterword

So if you've made it to the end, I assume I didn't anger you too much by dismissing one of your pet conspiracy theories or cause you to put the book in the microwave to destroy the trackers the government put into the binding.

You might have been surprised I didn't tear down all conspiracy theories as irrational, but rather, I pointed out how some are likely, while others are impossible. My goal wasn't to convince you that secret plans and cover-ups never happen or that you should always believe the official account of events.

Skepticism is healthy when done in a critical thinking way. But belief in irrational or impossible conspiracies is not only nonproductive, but it also opens a Pandora's box by which you can be easily manipulated. Believing the impossible means believing in almost anything and that's the path the manipulators will take to mold your thinking and your beliefs and distract you from what's important.

Remember the suggestion that the government and the military create and promote conspiracies of UFOs and secret aliens to cover for sightings and leaks of actual experimental aircraft? The best way to distract from truth is to create a distracting and appealing conspiracy theory to divert your attention. Hopefully, I've given you some cognitive tools to see what's possible and what's not and apply a healthy dose of skeptical critical thinking to official stories and claims of conspiracy.

I hope you enjoyed what's in this book as much as I enjoyed bringing it to you. Did you find the code hidden in the book and the secret messages? If you did, you have too much time on your hands. Listening for secret messages in popular music played backward is much more entertaining. Besides, I didn't actually hide any code or secret messages in this book. I wouldn't do that to you.

Or would I?

INDEX

NUMBERS

4chan, 117, 120
8chan, 120

A

Abbey Road, 186, 189
"action movie syndrome," 112
Aldrin, Buzz, 64
Al-Qaeda, 84, 86
Andrew, Prince, 168, 178
Apollo program. *See* moon landing hoax.
Area 51 and extraterrestrial UFOs, 69–82
- aliens visiting us (timing of), 75
- assessment of theories, 81–82
- con artists, claim by, 71
- existence of UFOs (government's admission of), 76
- experimental aircraft, 72, 78–80
- Facebook event, 69
- Fata Morgana (atmospheric ducting), 74
- flying saucer (military project to develop), 80
- "flying saucer frenzy," 70
- Freedom of Information Act request, 72
- goals, 77–78
- media focus, 76
- multiple personality disorder, 74
- naming of Area 51, 71
- nicknames for Area 51, 71
- obsession with Area 51, 69
- obsession with the United States, 73
- power of suggestion, 73
- Project Aquatone, 79
- Project Blue Book (air force), 79
- project management approach, 75
- Project Mogul, 70
- Project 1794, 80
- promoting public misinformation (method of), 78
- Roswell, New Mexico (events in), 69
- secret operations, 78
- Starlink satellite program, 74, 76
- UFO (unidentified flying object) conspiracy theorists, 70
- U-2 spy plane, 79

Armstrong, Neil, 64–65
Arnold, Kenneth, 70
assault weapons ban (1994), 110–111

B

Bay of Pigs Invasion (1961), 53
The Beatles, 185–186
Bernstein, Carl, 17
Biden, Joe, 22, 45, 123, 127
Big Pharma, 42, 141–144, 147
Bilderberg, 156–157, 159
bin Laden, Osama, 86, 87
birth rate, global, 140
Bowles, Camilla Parker, 164

brainwashing, 20, 108–109, 122
Brazel, W.W., 69–71
Bush, George H.W., 45, 57–58, 124, 156, 181
Bush, George W., 15, 57, 85, 111, 156, 158

C

Castro, Fidel, 21, 53, 54, 57, 86
celebrities, secretly murdered. *See* deep state and secretly murdered celebrities.
Charles, Prince, 164–165
chemtrails, 37–43
  cognitive closure, need for, 38
  creation of effect, 37–38
  data comparison, 41
  grounding of aircraft following 9/11, 41
  logic flaw, 42
  mind control, 42
  Occam's razor, 43
  plan considerations, 40
  problems, 39–40
  project management approach, 37, 39, 42
  trend in conspiracies, 42
CIA, 17–20, 49, 54, 57, 58, 71, 109, 119, 181
Clinton, Bill, 15, 116, 168, 178
Clinton, Hillary, 15, 116, 120, 122, 124, 128, 130, 158
"Clinton Body Count," 179–80
cognitive biases, 24
cognitive closure, need for, 23, 38
cognitive and psychological influences, 23–30
  acceptance, 26
  agreeableness, 27
  anchor questions, 28
  biases, 24–25
  "Big Five" measures," 26–27
  brain functioning, 28
  cognitive closure, need for, 23
  conscientiousness, 27
  cultivation theory, 29
  deception, 24
  defense of beliefs, 25
  delusional disorder, role of, 26
  extraversion, 27
  needs filled by conspiracies, 24
  neuroticism/emotional stability, 27
  9/11 conspiracies, belief in, 26
  openness, 27
  paranormal belief, 27
  schema, 25
  trusted authority and media, 24
Cold War, 8, 22, 55, 61, 156
condensation trails. *See* chemtrails.
confirmation bias, 24, 158
Connally, John, 47, 52–53
conspiracy theories, fascination with, 7–10
  internet use, 5
  project management, 8
  questions about, 8
  real-world events (1970s), 8
  spectrum of conspiracies, 9
conspiracy theories, spectrum of. *See* project management approach, spectrum of conspiracy theories and.
COVID-19 and COVID vaccines, 22, 42, 123, 131–151
  anti-vax movement, 141
  Big Pharma, vaccines as tool by (to make money), 141–144
    flaw in vaccine conspiracy theories, 142
    pharmaceutical companies (reality of), 144
    tale of two cautions, 143
  biological weapon meant to reduce world population (COVID-19 as), 137–141
    assumption as fact, 139
    attempted genocide, 141
    fear of overpopulation, 139
    fit with criteria, 138
    global birth rate, 140
    plot hole, 138
    starvation, 139

bioweapon released by China (COVID as), 136–137
boosters, 148
conspiracy flaws, 149
contradictory theories, (people supporting), 133
cultivation theory, 150
deaths from vaccine, 147–148
"dictator motivation," 149
first vaccines, 133
hoax (COVID-19 as), 133–136
goal of hoax conspiracy, 135
government methods of control, 135
on irrational side of the spectrum, 134, 135
"losing freedom", 136
presidential election, 134
ineffectiveness of, 145–146
meaning of term, 131
MERS, 132
MMR (mumps, measles, and rubella) vaccine, 144
motivation to believe conspiracies, 150–151
politicizing of the illness, 133
project management approach, 142–143
rush to approval, 145
SARS, 132
SARS-CoV-2, 131, 132
shutdown of schools and businesses, 133, 135
timeline of spread (phylogenetic algorithm), 132
tracking chips (vaccine contains), 146–147
Trump administration's response to the pandemic, 133
trypanophobia, 150
uncooperative people and anti-vaxxers (COVID-19 and vaccines meant to identify), 148–149
vaccine conspiracies, 141
crisis actors
anchor question about, 28
false flag events staged by, 98
important point about conspiracy theories involving, 106–107
paid (survivors and witnesses as), 114
problem with, 97
Sandy Hook as example of, 12
staging a mass shooting with, 14
Cuban Missile Crisis (1962), 53, 55–56, 61
cultivation theory, 29, 96, 150

D–E

Dean, John, 13
deep state and secretly murdered celebrities, 153–184
Bilderberg, 156–157, 159
"Clinton Body Count" or "Hillary Hit List," 179–180
death of Jeffrey Epstein, 168–178
arrest and murder planned in advance (conspiracy), 174–175
background, 168
coincidences, 170
conspiracies floating around, 170
incriminating videos, 169
murder (conspiracy), 172–174
plea deal with authorities (conspiracy), 177–178
sex trafficking (first legal complaints associated with), 168
staged suicide (conspiracy), 175
suicide (conspiracy), 170–172
suicide watch, 169
death of Marilyn Monroe (by the Kennedys), 162–163
death of Princess Diana (British royal family's orchestration of), 163–167
deep state
chemtrails and, 40
definition of, 14, 153

Donald Trump as enemy of, 159
manipulation of election outcomes, 160
murder of famous people posing a threat to, 161
QAnon and, 115
deep state organization (feasibility of), 180–184
conspiracy and fiction versions (differences between), 182
mass media, 183
mega-wealth and mega-influence (creation of), 180
politicians, 181
deep state rumors and conspiracies (biggest manufacturer of), 184
Freemasons, 154–155
greatest flaw of deep state conspiracy theories (example of), 158
Illuminati, 155
Jerusalem Cross, 154
Knights Templar, 153–154
Masonic temple, 155
multibillionaires thought to be behind secret plans, 157
project management approach, 163, 166, 167, 174, 177, 180
propaganda (access to mechanisms of), 161
propaganda (manipulation of voters through), 160
secret societies, 153
Shriners, 154
Skull and Bones, 155
"Deep Throat," 17
Diana, Princess, 163–167, 189

Epstein, Jeffrey, 117, 168–178

F

false flags. *See* mass shootings, false flags, and the truthers.
Fayed, Dodi, 163, 167
fear
instilled by 9/11 attacks, 112
as motivator to believe conspiracies, 150
propaganda's creation of, 14
fearmongering, 110, 162
Felt, William Mark, 16, 119
Flight 93, 98
Floyd, George, 136, 158
Ford, Gerald, 12, 18, 49
Freemasons, 153, 154–155

G–J

Gates, Bill, 150, 157
gun culture, 112

"Hillary Hit List," 116, 179–180

Illuminati, 40, 155, 183

Jackson, Michael, 161, 191
Johnson, Lyndon B., 45, 48

K–L

Kaysing, Bill, 60, 67
Kennedy, Jacqueline, 162
Kennedy, John F., 61, 65
Kennedy, Robert F., 56, 57
Kennedy assassination, 21, 22, 45–58, 121
conspiracy sources (range of), 45
eyewitness accounts, 48
George H.W. Bush (possible motive of), 57–58
"magic bullet," 52
most realistic theory, 58
motorcade route, 46
official record, 46
organized crime (possible motive of), 56–57
Oswald, shots fired by, 47
Oswald as fall guy, 52
project management approach, 49, 55
release of documents (delayed), 45
secret service (theories critical of), 50

Soviet Union and Cuba (possible motives of), 53–54
suggestion of brainwashing in, 108
umbrella conspiracy (Oswald), 51
Vice President Lyndon B. Johnson (possible motive of), 53
Warren Commission, 47–48, 54
Knights Templar, 153–154
Kubrick, Stanley, 65

Lanza, Adam, 103
Las Vegas shooting (2017), 104–106
Lavigne, Avril, 189–190
Lennon, John, 161, 186, 188, 189, 191, 192

M

Magical Mystery Tour, 186
mass shootings, false flags, and the truthers, 101–114
"action movie syndrome," 112
assault weapons ban (1994), 110–111
brainwashing, 108–109
crisis actors
false flag events staged by, 98
important point about conspiracy theories involving, 106–107
paid (survivors and witnesses as), 114
eternal three-step model of getting people to follow you, 110
false flag event (definition of), 101
false flags (conspiracy theories wrapped around), 101
fear (instilled by 9/11 attacks), 112
Las Vegas shooting (2017), 104–106
National Rifle Association (perception of), 113
Operation Northwoods (as false flag operation), 101
political propaganda, 110, 111
project management approach, 106, 107, 113
propaganda (gun promotion through), 111–112
safety, emotional need for (guns representing), 111–112
Sandy Hook Elementary School, 103–104, 107
three monkeys (image of), 102
truthers, 98
big push by, 103
description of, 102
target of, 105
Maxwell, Ghislaine, 168, 173
McCartney, Paul, 185, 186
McDougal, James (Jim), 116
Mitchell, John, 13
Monroe, Marilyn, 162
moon landing hoax, 59–68
Apollo program
origination of, 59
suspicions around validity of (book detailing), 60, 67
camera effect, 63–64
conspiracy contradicting itself, 65
Kennedy's challenge, 61, 65
logical explanations for supposed mysteries, 63
number of people needed to carry off conspiracy, 66
popularity of theory, 59
project management approach, 61, 65–68
tactic, 62
Watergate, impact of, 60

N–O

National Rifle Association (NRA), 113
National Security Agency (NSA), 119

9/11. *See* September 11, 2001.
Nixon, Richard, 12
Notorious B.I.G., 191
NRA. *See* National Rifle Association.
NSA. *See* National Security Agency.

Obama, Barack, 111, 122, 123, 158, 179
Occupy Wall Street movement, 158
Open Society Foundations, 157
Operation Bingo, 21
Operation Dirty Trick, 21
Operation Mongoose, 21
Operation Northwoods, 20–23, 54, 83, 101
  description of, 20–21
  as false flag operation, 101
  as good cover-up, 22
  how a secret became public knowledge, 21
  planned release of documents (delayed), 22
  plans rejected, 107
  project management approach, 21
  related proposals, 21
Oswald, Lee Harvey, 15, 45–58, 108

P

Paddock, Stephen, 105–106
Paul, Henri, 163, 166
Pentagon (9/11 attack on), 87, 93, 96–99
Pizzagate, 117
political propaganda, 110, 111
pop culture conspiracy theories, 185–197
  celebrities who faked their deaths to live normal, anonymous lives, 191–192
    Elvis Presley, 191
    flaws with theory, 192
    John Lennon, 191
    Michael Jackson, 191
    Notorious B.I.G., 191
    Tupac Shakur, 191
  famous people who died and were replaced by look-alikes, 185–191
    Avril Lavigne, 189–190
    Miley Cyrus, 190
  government monitoring of you through electronic devices, 195–196
  National Football League (scripting of), 194–195
  New Coke as cover to hide formula change in Classic Coke, 192–194
  project management approach, 187, 188, 190, 191, 193, 196
  replacement of birds with government spy drones, 196–197
power of suggestion, 73
Presley, Elvis, 161, 191
Project Aquatone, 79
project management approach
  Area 51 and extraterrestrial UFOs, 75
  chemtrails, 37, 39, 42
  COVID-19 and COVID vaccines, 142, 143
  deep state and secretly murdered celebrities, 163, 166, 167, 174, 177, 180
  Kennedy assassination, 49, 55
  mass shootings, false flags, and the truthers, 106, 107, 113
  moon landing hoax, 61, 65–68
  Operation Northwoods, 21
  pop culture conspiracy theories, 187, 188, 190, 191, 193, 196
  QAnon and the 2020 presidential election, 116, 125
project management approach, spectrum of conspiracy theories and, 11–16
  crisis actors, rule of thumb regarding, 12

dismissal of detail, 14
perception of threat, 15
project management approach, 13–15
questions to ask, 13
rational base to conspiracy theories, 11
spectrum of conspiracy theories, 11–13
suspension of disbelief, 12
Project MK-Ultra, 17–20
accusations, 18, 19
Executive Order 11905 and, 19
LSD, experiments studying the effects of, 17
psychedelics as weapon against government propaganda, 20
rule of thumb, 18
Project Mogul, 70
Project 1794, 80
propaganda, 8, 113, 117
access to mechanisms of, 161
Clintons as target of, 115
Cold War, 61
false flag events as, 101
government (psychedelics as weapon against), 20
guns promotion through, 111–112
manipulation of voters through, 160
political, 110, 111
websites (evolution of "Hillary Hit List" on), 179
psychology of conspiracy, 11–30
cognitive and psychological influences, 23–30
acceptance, 26
agreeableness, 27
anchor questions, 28
biases, 24–25
"Big Five" measures," 26–27
brain functioning, 28
cognitive closure, need for, 23
conscientiousness, 27
cultivation theory, 29
deception, 24
defense of beliefs, 25
delusional disorder, role of, 26
extraversion, 27
needs filled by conspiracies, 24
neuroticism/emotional stability, 27
9/11 conspiracies, belief in, 26
openness, 27
paranormal belief, 27
schema, 25
trusted authority and media, 24
environmental influences, 11
Operation Northwoods, 20–23
description of, 20–21
as good cover-up, 22
how a secret became public knowledge, 21
planned release of documents (delayed), 22
project management approach, 21
related proposals, 21
Project MK-Ultra, 17–20
accusations, 18, 19
Executive Order 11905 and, 19
LSD, experiments studying the effects of, 17
psychedelics as weapon against government propaganda, 20
rule of thumb, 18
smart conspiracies, 15–17
beliefs about the Clintons, 15
invasion of Iraq (Bush), 15
logic of Watergate, 16
ways of ignoring plot holes, 16
Tuskegee Study, 23
Watergate, 11–15
break-in attempts, 12, 13
covering their tracks, 15
criteria as good plan, 12, 13
deep state, 14
original group of burglars, 13
overconfidence, 14
plan failures, 13–14
sequence of events, 12
ultimate goal, question of, 13

Q–R

QAnon and the 2020 presidential election, 34, 115–130
conspiracy media, 118
cult, QAnon as, 122
death of JFK Jr., 121
death of Jim McDougal, 116–117
Deep State, 115
Edward Snowden, 119
"Hillary Hit List," 116
Pizzagate, 117
project management approach, 116, 125
propaganda (Clintons as target of), 115
"Q"
birthplace of, 117
postings from, 119–120
as real person, 121
roots of QAnon, 115
"secret insider information," 118
2020 presidential election, 123–130
claims of evidence, 129
election fraud conspiracies (roots of), 124
equal and opposite conspiracy theory, 130
"global elite," 125
political psychology, 123
results, 127
social media (as drivers of conspiracy belief), 125
"stolen election" conspiracy (criteria violated by), 128
voter fraud (claims of), 123–130
Democrats and Republicans (voting choices of), 123–124
rationality of plan, 127
stuffing ballots, 126
vote-by-mail system (attitudes toward), 123–124

Red Scare, 14
Rockefeller Commission, 18
Ruby, Jack, 48, 49, 56

S

Sandy Hook Elementary School, 6, 103–104, 107, 111
SARS-CoV-2 (Severe Acute Respiratory Syndrome CoronaVirus 2), 131
secret service, theories critical of, 50
September 11, 2001, 83–99
Al-Qaeda, 84, 86
building collapse (erroneous reports of), 94
conspiracies, belief in, 26
conspiracy theories, suspension of disbelief, 12
controlled demolition, 9, 14, 38, 89–91, 94–95
crisis actors
false flag events staged by, 98
problem with, 97
cultivation theory, 96
deal-breaker question, 91
early misreporting, 85
empty planes theory, 99
false reports, 85
Flight 93, 87–88
goal of the conspiracy, 92
grounding of commercial aircraft following, 41
"inside job" (belief in), 83
live TV, 87, 93
low collateral damage argument, 87
missile theory (against Pentagon), 97, 98
most common cut-and-paste chant, 95
official account, 83–84
Pentagon, 87, 93, 96–99
rational theories, 85–86
Taliban, 86
Twin Towers and 7 WTC, 89
WTC towers ("tube within a tube" design of), 90
Sgt. Pepper's Lonely Hearts Club Band, 185, 187

Shakur, Tupac, 191
The Shriners, 154
Skull and Bones, 153, 155, 181
smart conspiracies, 15–17
    beliefs about the Clintons, 15
    invasion of Iraq (Bush), 15
    logic of Watergate, 16
    ways of ignoring plot holes, 16
Snowden, Edward, 119, 195
social media (as drivers of conspiracy belief), 125
Soros, George, 157, 158
SpaceX, 74
suspicion, as motivator to believe conspiracies, 150

T-U-V

Taliban, 86
Tripp, Linda, 15
Trump, Donald, 22, 45, 117, 121, 123, 125, 127, 128, 130, 133, 134, 158, 159, 168, 178
truthers. *See* mass shootings, false flags, and the truthers.
Tuskegee Study, 23
2020 presidential election. *See* QAnon and the 2020 presidential election.

UFO (unidentified flying object) conspiracy, 70
U-2 spy plane, 79

Vandella, Melissa, 189
vapor trails. *See* chemtrails.

W

Warren Commission, 58
    creation of, 48
    investigation of organized crime by, 57
    investigation of Soviet Union and Cuba by, 54
    report from, 47
Watergate, 2, 11–17, 60, 119, 163
    break-in attempts, 12–13
    conspiracy theories becoming mainstream due to, 163
    covering their tracks, 15
    criteria as good plan, 12, 13
    deep state, 14
    impact on growing cultural awareness in the 1970s, 60
    logic of, 16
    original group of burglars, 13
    overconfidence, 14
    plan failures, 13–14
    sequence of events, 12
    ultimate goal, question of, 13
weapons of mass destruction, as justification for invasion of Iraq, 15
White Album, 186
Whitewater investigation, 115, 116
WHO. *See* World Health Organization.
Woodward, Bob, 17
World Health Organization (WHO), 132, 137
World Trade Center (WTC), 83

ABOUT THE AUTHOR

Casey Lytle has been teaching psychology and sociology for more than a decade at the university and community college levels. He's designed and taught classes in the psychology of deception, the psychology of murder, human sexuality, and the effects of trauma on memory. Student interest in conspiracy theories led to his project management approach to conspiracies and placing them on a spectrum to separate the rational from the irrational. In 2021, Casey started making short TikTok videos introducing psychology and sociology topics. His videos have collected more than 10 million views. Casey lives in the Pacific Northwest with his son and a collection of creepy dolls.

ACKNOWLEDGMENTS

There are several key individuals who helped me end up in the right place and right time to get this book written and published. In chronological order: My aunt and uncle in Bellingham, Washington, who hosted the get-together in 1961 where I was accidentally conceived. My oldest brother, Richard Lytle, who saved me from the abyss multiple times. Professor Mark Holland, who primed me for success on my late-life return to school. My son, Vincent, who has been the motivation to keep going and has probably been more of a role model for me than I've been for him. My graduate studies chair, Dr. Kayleen Islam-Zwart, and department chair, Theresa Martin, both at Eastern Washington University, who set my path and gave me the opportunity to teach psychology. Natalie Peters, who encouraged me to create a professional online presence. Mike Sanders at DK Publishing, who found me in the haystack of online creators. And, of course, my editors: Alexandra Andrzejewski and Christopher Stolle, who did the hard work of turning my in-class conversational style of writing into something readable and made the entire process easy and transparent on my end.